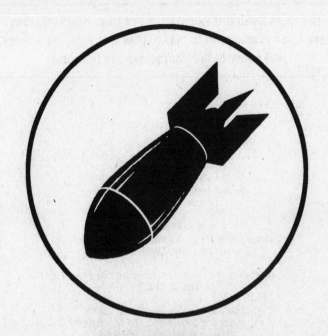

TERRY
DEARY'S
TERRIBLY TRUE
WAR STORIES

SCHOLASTIC

The facts behind these stories are true. However, they have been dramatized to make them into gripping stories, and some of the characters are fictitious.

Scholastic Children's Books,
Euston House, 24 Eversholt Street
London, NW1 1DB, UK

A division of Scholastic Ltd
London ~ New York ~ Toronto ~ Sydney ~ Auckland
Mexico City ~ New Delhi ~ Hong Kong

First published in the UK under the series title *True Stories* by
Scholastic Ltd, 1997

Typeset by Rapid Reprographics Ltd
Printed by Nørhaven Paperback A/S, Denmark

10 9 8 7 6 5 4 3 2 1

CONTENTS

INTRODUCTION

From 1992 till 1994 I was manager of a military museum. It proudly displayed the weapons, the medals, the flags and the photographs of the local regiment.

The most popular display in the whole museum was about a man who won the Victoria Cross. He seemed to be a great hero. But one of the staff at the museum told me a curious story of something that happened 40 years after the hero had won his medal.

It shows that stories of war are not simply about death and destruction and machines. They are about people. People ... and how they behave when they are suddenly faced with the strangest human invention of all.

War.

I won't forget the story of Eric Mohn and Alan Wakefield. This is it ...

Date: February 1985
Place: A military museum in the north of England

The museum was quiet and dust settled on the war machines. The guns and tanks and gloomy glass cases stood as silent as the memories inside them. Memories of battles and memories of the people who fought in them. Ageing photographs had frozen the

8

faces of soldiers and their broken battlefields forever. The place was more like a graveyard than a military museum.

A woman walked in, her low heels tapping softly on the cold floor. She stopped in front of a small field gun. It was battered and scarred underneath its coat of fresh brown paint. There was a wall display behind the gun and it told the story behind it. "Alan Wakefield's gun" it said.

There was a photograph of Wakefield, a smirking, hard-faced young man in a British Army uniform with the cap tilted at a jaunty angle. Next to the picture was a small case with a lid of armour-plated glass; inside hung a brass medal with a purple ribbon and a neatly typed label that said, "Alan Wakefield's Victoria Cross". There was a copy of an old newspaper article that told the story of how he'd won the medal.

Before the woman could finish reading it an old museum attendant strolled along the gallery towards her. He stopped at her side and smiled, pleased to have a visitor to talk to on this wintry day. "Reading about Alan Wakefield, eh?"

"Yes."

"Our most famous Victoria Cross," the man said. He leaned forward and wiped a faint fingerprint from the armour-plated glass.

The woman was staring at the photograph and the hard-faced hero stared back at her. She said nothing.

The attendant went on, "He was in the North African desert in 1942 when the German army was driving us back."

"Ah," she said. "You were there?"

"No. I was back here in England working in the pit to dig the coal to help the war effort," he explained.

"Ah," she nodded.

"I was only 16," he said. "Anyway, Alan Wakefield was given the job of holding back a German attack with this gun while the rest of the army escaped to safety. When the first German tank appeared on the road he hit it. The tank burst into flames and blocked the road. The Germans were held up. Of course they were annoyed and brought up another tank to blow him out of the way. The first shot killed three of the crew and wounded Wakefield."

"Oh, so there were others there too?" the woman said quietly.

"Well, yes. You can't fire one of these on your own. There was a crew of five. But after that tank attack there were just two left. The aimer and the loader, Wakefield. Now, even though he was wounded Wakefield kept loading the gun. He hit the second tank and held the Germans up for even longer."

"That was good aiming," the woman said, and there was a faint smile on her face.

"The next German shell hit Wakefield's ammunition. It killed the aimer and blew Wakefield's arm off. And do you know what he did?"

"It says here that he began to crawl back to the gun with

another shell in his remaining arm," the woman said, peering at the newspaper report through heavy glasses.

"He did," the attendant said proudly. "And in this case we have the very shell he was carrying when a final shell killed him. And that's the Victoria Cross they presented to Wakefield's widow."

The woman's eyes strayed to the winter parkland outside the museum and two ducks slithering across the frozen pond. "My brother fought in the war," she said.

"Really? Which regiment?" the attendant asked. Over the years he'd learned to judge people by who they fought with.

"With this regiment. The Sixth Battalion," she said.

"Really? The same as Wakefield then!"

"My brother was a gentle man. He didn't hate anyone and he'd never fought in his life before he joined the regiment. He didn't find it easy."

"No. The army can be a hard life," the attendant said, and he straightened his back. He'd joined the regiment shortly after the war. He'd survived.

"The main problem was he was bullied," the woman explained. "He was doing a good job. He was a very skilled soldier. But he did not get on with all the other men. He was a bit shy, I suppose. He enjoyed reading. One of the men could not read. That man picked on my brother constantly. Eric's letters home broke my heart."

The attendant nodded, not sure what to say. "Have you checked his war record with the office upstairs? They may be able to give you some details. What is his name?"

"Thank you. They gave us details when he died. His name was Eric Mohn," she said softly. A flicker of a frown crossed the attendant's face.

"Mohn ... but..."

"We are from a Dutch family but the name sounds German. That is what the bully taunted poor Eric with. His name. His love of reading. His inability to fist-fight. He showed Eric how to fist-fight by punching him every chance he had."

"I'm sorry," the attendant said.

"Eric was one of five men who died one afternoon," she said. "He had been given the job of stopping a German tank advance in the North African desert," she explained. "He was a gun aimer. He was wonderful at his job. He had no hatred in his heart – no fighting spirit – but he fought bravely and hit a German tank with his first shot. The Germans fought back and killed three of his friends. He was wounded but kept firing. For all the death and destruction around him he kept his nerve. His next shot hit another German tank."

The woman walked towards the small, freshly-painted field gun and rested a hand on the cold barrel. "The other man left alive was just a labourer. Not a very bright man. But he was useful for carrying shells. A strong man. A violent man. A bully, in fact. The bully who had made Eric so desperately unhappy he wanted to shoot himself."

The attendant's face was pale and only a small muscle twitched in his cheek. The woman touched the glass case with the medal inside. "So isn't it strange that they gave a medal to the bully who went on hating – even after his arm was blown off. But our Eric, who fought bravely and skilfully in the face of a German advance, only got a sandy grave? Why is that, do you think?"

The attendant cleared his throat. "Strange things happen in war, madam," he said.

"Yes," she agreed. "And war stories are not about guns and tanks and shells and medals. They are about people like my brother. And about the people left behind to hope – to suffer – to mourn. They are about people like me."

She looked at the faded copy of the newspaper on the wall. "When will they learn? War stories are not just about action. They are about feelings too."

The attendant had no answer.

The woman turned and the tapping of her heels faded as she walked out of the museum doors and on to the frosty path.

The museum was quiet and dust settled on the war machines. The place was more like a graveyard than a military museum.

BEATEN

War makes people behave in strange ways. It tests their courage. Some people are threatened and act more bravely than anyone could ever believe. Others will do anything to save their miserable skins. They will even betray innocent children in their care. That's what happened in a war that the Romans fought against the Etruscans...

Date: 394 BC
Place: Falerii, Etruria, north-eastern Italy

I remember the day the Romans came to Falerii. It was many years ago now and I was just a boy in school. We had no fear at all. Only a sense of excitement that something had come to take the boredom from our lives.

We didn't think. We didn't know that the Romans could kill our parents and make us slaves. In fact, even if they'd told us, we'd have said, "So what? We're already slaves in Master Marcellus's school." The boys called him the slave driver. He taught us Maths and Geography and History and tested us mercilessly. One by one we had to stand in front of the class, tunics rolled down to the waist, while he asked us questions about the morning's lessons. One mistake and he brought a cane down on your back.

They say he used to be a wrestler and killed a man in a contest. We all wondered who would be the first of his pupils to be killed by his beatings.

Then the Romans came. "Why?" I asked my friend Lucius.

"We stand in the way of their trade routes to the north," he explained. His father was a minister to the king and knew everything. "The Romans want us to pay tribute to them. The king refuses."

"What will the Romans do?" I wondered. I was younger than Lucius and knew less about the ways of war.

"The Romans won't do anything," he smirked. "We have the finest javelin throwers, axe soldiers and archers in the world. We will crush them."

"But what about if they crush *us*, Lucius?" I asked.

"They won't, Tarquin," he promised. "If you don't believe me, ask Master Marcellus."

"Ask him what?" a voice said softly. I jumped, as I always did when the teacher appeared.

"Nothing, sir!" I squeaked.

But Lucius was braver than I and he said, "Tarquin is wondering what will happen if the Romans defeat us?"

The teacher had a hard-edged, strong-jawed face with eyes set so deep that you could never read his thoughts. "The Romans will probably kill all the fighting men and turn the women and children into slaves," he said.

"So we're not in danger of being killed," Lucius said.

The teacher leaned forward and breathed in our faces. His breath smelled like the rat our dog once brought into the house and hid under a couch. "You are not. But *I* am."

"But you're not afraid, sir, are you?" Lucius asked brightly.

The teacher gripped my friend's shoulder so hard that his

knuckles turned white. "How dare you suggest it, Lucius Quintus."

"I didn't!" he cried.

"In fact," the teacher went on. "I will show you my courage. I will leave the city this afternoon and I will run around the walls, the way we do every afternoon."

"The Romans are camped around the walls," I gasped.

"I will kill any Roman who tries to stop me," the teacher boasted. "With my bare hands," he added.

I looked at the hands like knotted oak and I believed him. "Can we watch?" I asked. I turned to Lucius. "Will your father give us permission to climb the walls and watch?"

Lucius was about to answer when Master Marcellus cut in, "There will be no need for that. You will all be coming with me!"

My mouth went dry at the thought. It was the most exciting thing I'd ever done. Suddenly I forgave Master Marcellus for all his beatings. I hurried into the classroom and spread the news to my classmates.

There were just 12 of us altogether in that class. The morning lessons passed in a fever of excitement. Even the teacher was caught up in the mood. I made three mistakes, waited for the lash of his cane on my back and felt nothing. I turned to watch him gazing out of the window with a grim smile on his thin lips. All he said was, "Yes, Tarquin, very good, Tarquin."

At three hours after noon, when the fierce heat of the sun was dropping, we stripped off our tunics and sandals and put on a loose loincloth. At the gates to Falerii we stopped and spoke to the captain of the guard. "The boys must have their exercise, Romans or no Romans," Master Marcellus said.

"The Romans won't hurt the boys," the captain nodded and opened a small door in the huge gate to let us out on to the plain.

The Romans had arrived the night before and their tents were in clusters about a mile from the walls, just out of reach of our catapults. Even a mile away we could hear the hammering and see the wooden war machines being put together. The Romans would never try a straight attempt at climbing the walls. They would batter us with boulders and storm the gates with battering rams and Greek fire before they risked their soldiers.

We set off at the usual running pace with Master Marcellus coming last to deliver a kick to any boy who began to fall behind. The enemy watched us with interest but made no move to capture us or even stop us for questioning. We kept close to our massive city walls and went round them in a complete circle.

An hour later we arrived back at the city gate. I was disappointed. I'd been on more dangerous fishing trips. The teacher's hard face was glowing with sweat and pride. "The Romans are afraid of me," he told us. "Tomorrow we will run halfway to their camp and see if they dare stop us."

"They'll probably run away!" Lucius laughed.

I scarcely slept that night, thinking about the adventure that lay ahead of us. But, again, the next day was a disappointment. We ran so close to the Roman camp that we could have thrown stones at their guards. Still nothing happened.

"Tomorrow we should go right up to their guards and challenge them to a fight!" Lucius cried when we got home that afternoon.

"They wouldn't fight with boys," Master Marcellus sneered.

Lucius frowned. "No, sir. I meant *you* could fight them. One at a time, of course."

"Of course," the teacher said with a tight smile. "We will certainly get close enough to twist a Roman nose or two," the teacher said. The boys cheered. Master Marcellus had never been so popular. I didn't cheer quite so loudly as the other boys.

"What's wrong, Tarquin?" he asked.

"I don't think I can reach up high enough to twist a Roman nose," I said.

The man grabbed me by the hair and lifted me clean off the ground. "Then we'll have to help you, little Tarquin!" he cried, and the boys roared with laughter.

He dropped me in the dust of the road and swished at my legs with his cane before he turned and walked off home.

That night I'll swear I did not sleep for even a moment. I was exhausted when the sun streamed through my window next morning, letting me know it was time for school. As we practised our writing on wax boards that morning, the teacher was writing in ink on a parchment scroll. Lucius walked boldly to the teacher's seat to ask for a new stylus and hurried back to the table. "He's writing a list of our names and who our parents are. He has 'Varius Quintus – senator in charge of the treasury' next to my name. That's my father."

"Why is he doing that?" I asked.

"I don't know," Lucius shrugged. "But he had sergeant of the guard against your father's name and a small star."

I didn't understand, but I did notice that Master Marcellus had the scroll of names in his hand when he lined us up at the gate that afternoon. This time he led the way and warned us to stay close behind him. He ran straight to the guard who stood on the road that led into the northern Roman camp. "Who is your leader?" he demanded.

The guard had his short sword unsheathed. He was so broad and tanned that he made our wrestling teacher look candle-thin and pale. I was sure he would stab the first boy to reach for his nose. "Camillus," he grunted.

"Then I want you to tell Camillus that I have a gift for him."

The guard looked unsure but went to an officer for advice. The officer waved a hand and beckoned for us to follow him. Master

Marcellus was whistling as he stepped lightly through the Roman tents to the largest and finest one, which seemed to be made of silk. A Roman in a purple toga stepped out of the tent; he was older than the other soldiers, with grey hair and a thin nose. He looked down that nose at our teacher who seemed to shrivel just a little under the gaze. "What do you want?"

"I'm a teacher," Master Marcellus said. "And these are my pupils."

"So?"

Our master pulled the scroll from under his arm and unrolled it. "You will see that their fathers are important men in the city. Lucius there has a father in the treasury," he said in a soft and whining voice. He turned and his eye fell on me. "Tarquin here has a father on guard at the west gate. The fathers love their sons. They wouldn't want to see them hurt," our teacher went on.

It took me some time to understand what was happening. In fact it took Camillus the Roman to explain. "It's a fine teacher you have here, boys. He is offering you to the Romans as a gift!"

"A very rich gift," Master Marcellus went on quickly. "Take the boys back to the main gate with a knife at every throat. See how quickly the gates will open. You won't have to fight at all!"

"He's a traitor," Lucius whispered to me.

Camillus tugged at his purple toga and pulled it closer around him as if he felt a shiver. "Of course, master teacher, you would want something in return."

"Only spare my life," Master Marcellus said with a soft whinge and a bent head.

Camillus tilted his head back and looked down the full length of his eagle nose. The nostrils looked pinched as if he had a bad smell beneath them. "War is a terrible thing, but at least there are rules that brave men will follow. And brave men will fight for victory against other brave men. We do not take it from the jaws of some slavering dog who trades for his miserable life with children."

"Then you don't want to accept my offer?" Master Marcellus gasped.

"I would rather die on the end of an Etruscan sword than live with a knife to a child's throat," the Roman general said.

"But what am I to do?" the teacher gasped. "I can't go back!"

"You will go back," Camillus said. He nodded to two of his guards. "Bind this man's hands behind his back," he ordered.

"I thought I was doing something that Rome would be grateful for!" the teacher wailed.

Camillus ignored him as the guards found a length of rope and bound his hands. When Camillus took the soldier's sword Master Marcellus dropped to his knees and began to cry softly. Camillus gripped the neck of the teacher's tunic, raised the sword and slashed the cloth neatly down the centre of the back. He tugged at the sleeves till they fell down to the tied wrists. Then, he grabbed the teacher by the hair and pulled him to his feet.

He called for a centurion to bring a bundle of canes and he

counted out 12. "We use these to punish soldiers," he explained to us and walked amongst us handing them out. "Now, boys, this teacher says he will not go back to Falerii. But if you take turns in beating him every time he stops, then he may change his mind."

We looked at the canes, bewildered. Lucius was the first to raise his. "He's beaten us often enough," he said. "But we don't want revenge, do we?"

"Yes," I said.

My friend glared at me. "No. We are not doing this for revenge. We are doing this because he's a traitor who must be taken to judgement," he said and brought the cane down sharply on the teacher's back.

The teacher screamed and started hurrying down the path back to the city. I looked at the cane in my hand and remembered the times that something like this had beaten me till I bled and had to sleep face down for days. "We're not doing this for revenge," I said seriously to Lucius as we trotted after our classmates.

"Not *entirely* revenge," Lucius said.

"But a little bit, perhaps?"

Lucius gave a sudden grin and broke into a run to catch up to the others. "Maybe just a little bit!" he admitted.

Traitors

The teacher was punished twice. When Master Marcellus returned to the city, whipped and bleeding, he was executed for betraying his own people.

War stories are interesting because we can look at how people behave when they are faced with death. We can try to guess how we would behave in the same situation. Would we die bravely or betray everything just to save our lives?

Many people can forgive an enemy – after all they are fighting for their lives just the same. But those same people hate a *traitor*. Traitors have existed in every age and some have survived better than others...

1. In AD 67 the Jewish defenders of Jotapata believed they should die rather than surrender to the Romans. Their leader, Josephus, disagreed, but he was outvoted and they threatened to kill him. Thinking quickly, Josephus said suicide was wrong but suggested that they should kill one another by drawing lots. Of the 32 defenders one half would kill the other half and leave just 16. The 16 would draw lots again, half would kill the other half and leave eight ... and again to leave four and again to leave two. By chance (or by some trick) one of the last two was the leader Josephus who didn't want to die. He made a deal with the other survivor and they both lived. Their 30 dead comrades would have felt betrayed!

F A C T

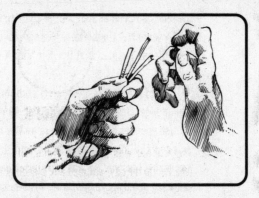

F I L E

2. Running away from a battle, or deserting, has always been punished harshly. If a Roman soldier deserted his company then his comrades would punish him by stoning him to death. If the whole company ran away then it was "decimated" – they drew lots to see who would be unlucky and one man in ten was executed.

3. Failing to obey orders has also been seen as betrayal and harshly punished in the past. A Chinese warrior was told to wait for the order to attack. But he rode out alone and came back with the heads of two enemy soldiers. The warrior's emperor, Wu Ch'i, had him beheaded for disobeying orders. A Roman general called Manlius had a similar problem when one of his soldiers killed an enemy before he was ordered to. Manlius had the Roman hero executed … even though it was his own son!

4. In England in 1439, King Henry VI was the first to pass a law against deserting. By 1639 a soldier could be hanged for selling the weapons he was given or even for complaining about his commander! Soldiers who swore may have had a red-hot poker pushed through their tongues. By 1712 the death penalty had been abandoned for some time, but over a period of 14 years one troublesome gunner received 25,000 lashes! (His friends reported that this left him "hearty and well".)

5. One of the world's most famous traitors was the American commander Benedict Arnold. He sold American secrets to the British enemies during the American War of Independence. He needed the money because he and his wife enjoyed an expensive lifestyle. He was also upset because younger men were promoted above him. When his treason was uncovered he joined the British Army and fought for them against his own countrymen. But, when the war was over, the British were disgusted by his treason and gave him very poor reward.

6. In World War I the punishment for deserting was to be shot by a firing squad. Executions usually took place at dawn, the day after the deserter was found guilty. The firing squad would have six rifles, one with a "blank" bullet in, so each man in the firing squad could believe that he hadn't shot the victim. Other soldiers were shot for giving away passwords and falling asleep when on guard duty.

7. By World War II the death sentence for deserting had been abolished. No British soldiers were shot for this crime. But Britain's most hated traitor in this war was William Joyce – a man who never even fought for the enemy. What Joyce did was broadcast radio messages to the British people giving them bad news and telling them they may as well give up because they would lose. His posh voice earned him the nickname "Lord Haw-Haw". It also betrayed him – as he tried to hide in a group of refugees after the war he was recognized because of his voice. He was caught and executed. Some people think he was a little unlucky because he wasn't British – he was American – so he could not really be accused of treason.

8. One group of British soldiers who are usually forgotten are the "British Free Corps". They fought for the German army in World War II. John Amery was the founder of this corps, even though his father was a minister in the British Government. He visited prisoner-of-war camps and tried to persuade captured British soldiers to join him. After the war he said the Germans had forced him to do it. No one believed him and he was hanged.

CONQUERED

"*Wars*" *can go on for years, sometimes with long periods when there is no fighting. But "battles" are usually over in a few hours. And in those hours one moment can decide the winner. That moment can change the course of the battle, change the course of the war and change the history of a nation. The Battle of Hastings is a famous example. Most people are sure it was an arrow in King Harold's eye that changed the course of the battle. It wasn't quite that simple...*

Date: 14 October 1066
Place: Hastings, southern England

The woman stood on the edge of the wood and looked at the moonlit valley below her. For a moment she thought her house was still on fire, but she knew it couldn't be. Not after a week.

Smoke was drifting upwards in the still air. The mud and wattle walls were firm enough. She'd laboured weeks with her husband, Wulf, to make them thick and strong. But the roof had burnt away leaving blackened timbers like a charred skeleton.

She muttered the old rhyme that her mother had taught her. It had been about the ruin of the Roman kingdom when the Saxons took over. "Wondrous are the walls, wrecked by fate; the buildings crumble, roofs have caved in, towers collapse; barred gates are broken; houses are gaping, tottering and fallen; death removed every brave man." Now she was looking at the ruin of the Saxon village since the Normans arrived.

The Normans had set fire to it a week ago. They had been very careful about their task. First there was a hammering at the door. The soldiers who stood there were dressed in leather tunics with metal rings sewn on. They carried swords but no shields or helmets. They were not expecting any trouble.

"Leave the house," ordered the soldier who appeared to be in charge. He spoke in very poor Saxon.

"I speak French," the woman told him. "My husband trades with your country."

The soldier smiled. His dark hair was cropped shorter than the Saxons and he had no beard or moustache. "What is it, Oswyn?" Wulf called.

"The Normans," she replied.

Her husband had come to the door. A powerful man although he was over 40 years old now, his moustache turning grey and his long, fair hair growing thin.

The soldier gripped his sword a little tighter but didn't raise it. "Will you leave the house, sir. Duke William of Normandy has ordered it. I'm Sergeant Henri Caen."

"Duke William is not king of England," Oswyn said coolly.

The soldier shrugged. "He should be. Your King Harold swore that Duke William would become king when old Edward died. Your Harold broke his promise. That's why we are here."

"My family have farmed this land for three hundred years. They will farm it for William, Harold or whoever is king. Why not leave us alone?" Wulf asked. Oswyn knew her husband was brave in battle but he had no temper.

The soldier stuck the point of his sword in the ground and

dragged it over the damp earth. "The Duke explained it to us. We have landed here, near your port of Hastings. If we march north to meet your Harold then we'll be exhausted and he'll be waiting, ready to defend himself. But if we stay here then Harold has to march south to us. He'll be the tired one and we'll be the ones in a strong position, see?"

"And what if Harold doesn't walk into your trap? Why should he?" Oswyn asked.

"Harold won't stand by and watch the Normans burn his country to the ground," the soldier told her.

"You're planning to burn our buildings?"

"That's why we want you to leave."

Wulf and his son Edwin, who had joined him at the door, looked at the armed men. There was no point in sacrificing their lives to defend a home that would be burned anyway. Better to leave and join Harold for the battle that would come when their king arrived. "Can we take anything before you set fire to the house?"

"You'll need food ... but leave your weapons," the sergeant told them.

When they left, Oswyn had looked back only once. The roof had been blazing and the soldiers were driving off the best cattle. She didn't look back again but set off for the shelter of Manser's Wood.

Now the food had run out. She needed to go back to the grain pit where the year's harvest should have been safe from the fire. She had buried Wulf after searching the battlefield with the other women. But her son Edwin seemed to have escaped. Now she had to start rebuilding the farm for her son's return.

The smoke from the ruins came from a fire. A group of Norman soldiers huddled around a stone hearth. The walls sheltered them from the damp night air. She looked through the ruined doorway and the firelight glinted on the keys that she wore at her belt – keys to doors that were shattered and burned. The soldier jumped to his feet, suddenly afraid that the glint could be a dagger.

When he saw it was a middle-aged woman in a russet dress he smiled. "Good evening," he said.

Oswyn did not return the smile. "Sergeant Caen," she said. "It's a pity you burned the house. It doesn't give such good shelter now you need it."

"I remembered how strong the walls are. We're just resting the night here. We march on London tomorrow."

She swayed slightly and her eyes closed. He hurried forward, took her by the elbow and led her to a block of wood that served as a seat. "Sorry," she said. "The food ran out two days ago."

He helped her by tearing some of the rabbit that was roasting on a simple spit over the fire. She chewed at it hungrily, not caring about the grease that ran down her chin. "Your husband?" the sergeant asked.

"Killed in the battle," she said quietly.

"A lot of good men died," the Norman told her.

"We are Christians, of course," she told him. "But the old beliefs linger on. We still believe that a man who dies in battle goes straight to heaven."

"Aye," the soldier muttered. "I'm sure that's what happened

to your husband. He'll be a happy man."

Her face looked odd, lit on one side by cold moonlight and the other by warm firelight. "I would prefer it if my husband was miserable and alive and you were happy and dead," she said.

"I know," the sergeant said. "I have a wife back in Normandy. She would say the same if he had killed me."

"But he didn't. The Normans won."

"The Saxons fought bravely," the man told her.

"I know," she said. "I watched from Manser's Wood. I thought at one point you were beaten."

"I think perhaps we were," he nodded. "I mean we started badly. Harold marched quicker than Duke William imagined. He was up there on the ridge and waiting while we marched from Hastings."

"We call it Senlac Hill," the woman said.

"You can't ask men in chain mail to attack up hill for too long. No, Harold had the advantage there," he said.

"Ah, but he marched so fast he left most of his archers behind," Oswyn said.

Sergeant Caen spitted another rabbit and placed it over the fire. "We attacked with our archers first, the way we always do. But the enemy usually fires back and we pick up their arrows. Since your Harold hadn't many archers we soon ran out of arrows and the battle had hardly started."

"That's when you marched up Senlac Hill," the woman nodded.

"We did. God, but your Saxons are fearsome with their huge axes. We stabbed at them with our swords but we were never going to drive them off the hill. We lost men but at least we went back down the hill in good order. We didn't run away."

"I saw your knights attack," Oswyn nodded. "That was a foolish thing to do!"

"It was part of Duke William's plan!"

"No! It was part of King Harold's plan," the woman said with a grim smile. "He knows this valley. This is Harold's homeland. The land is swampy down there and the slope is too steep. The horses couldn't gallop up it. Your knights were being dragged down by the hundred. Don't tell me they didn't start running away that time."

The sergeant spread his hands. "That's when we thought the battle was lost. Our knights charged back towards us foot-soldiers and started to trample us. Duke William fell off his horse and the cry went up that he was dead. Some men were already running back to Hastings and the safety of the boats. We saw the Saxons charging down Senlac Hill to finish us off and a lot of us said our last prayers. Our courage went when our hope went."

"What happened?"

"A miracle," the man said, then he shook his head. "No, God forgive me, that's not true. It was not a holy miracle. It was just a very quick piece of thinking by Duke William. He rode to the top of a small mound and tore off his helmet so we could all see that he was still alive. Of course we rushed to his side and soon we were an army again. We turned and faced your Saxons. But this time we weren't fighting up Senlac Hill. Now we were fighting on the soft ground at the bottom. Our knights and our foot-soldiers all together. We were slipping in the mud – at times we were slipping in blood – but not one Saxon got back to the safety of the hilltop."

Oswyn rose to her feet and stared out through the broken door. She looked across to the place where that part of the battle had raged. "That's where Wulf fell," she said. "I watched him leading a group of local men down that hill. He died in the valley in that fight around the Duke."

"A lot of Normans died too."

She turned and looked back at him. "For what?"

"For a kingdom. For a kingdom. That was the moment when the battle turned. Harold *must* have told those men not to leave the hill. Once they charged down the hill after us – and once Duke William turned us to face them – the Saxons were lost. The kingdom was lost."

"But the battle didn't end," she said.

"No," he admitted. "We had broken some of Harold's bravest and best men, but he still had half an army on that hilltop. The sun had set and we still hadn't shifted your king from Senlac Hill." From his seat by the fire Sergeant Caen could look through the charred roof beams to the dark hill that stood in silhouette against the purple, starry sky.

He remembered that he was nearby when William gave the order for his archers to fire high into the air so they would drop out of the sky on to Harold and his remaining men. "They will have to raise their shields over their heads to shelter," Duke William had explained. "While they are sheltering under their shields, our Norman knights will make one more rush up the hill."

"The fresh attack by the archers worked," Sergeant Caen said. "They say that Harold himself was struck in the eye. He leaned on his shield in agony; his men might still have saved him but our knights were at the top of the hill by then. Four of them rode for Harold under his banner of the Fighting Man. When Harold was cut down the Saxons broke and fled."

"Some came past me in the woods," Oswyn said. "They fought till it grew too dark to fight any more."

"Yes, the dark saved a lot of Saxon lives."

"Perhaps it saved my Edwin's," the woman said.

"I hope so," the Norman said.

"Do you?"

"Of course. You will have a new king and a French baron will own your land. But we still need strong Saxons to work the land. If he does return then tell him to lay down his axe and his sword. William will be a good king to anyone who obeys. William of Normandy is an honourable man."

"Is he?"

Sergeant Caen turned the rabbit so the juices dropped into the fire and made it spit and flare bright orange. "Let me tell you about William. When Harold lay dead on the ridge a knight called Ivo began hacking at the body. William was ashamed that a noble enemy like Harold should be treated that way. Ivo has been sent back to Normandy in disgrace. The knights will share out the Angle and Saxon lands but Ivo won't get a hair's breadth."

"And what will happen to the people who fight on?" the woman asked.

"Then they will find Duke William is the cruellest king on this earth." The soldier lifted the smoking meat from the fire, cut a piece of the roasted flesh and offered it to the woman. She took it and began to chew it. "In a war you have to obey orders or die," he said.

She looked into the fire and nodded. "If my Wulf had obeyed – if he had stayed on the hill like Harold told him to – then he'd be alive now," she said.

"And I'd probably be dead," the Norman said.

"And Harold would be king." She sighed. "If only Wulf had obeyed."

The soldier stood up. "I'll leave you in peace in your own house," he said. "Tomorrow I'll send a troop of men to help put a roof back on."

"Why?" she asked. "I am one of the losers."

"Because soon after Wulf charged and Harold fell, you became a Norman. Now you are one of us. Now it is my duty to protect you. Life goes on."

"Not for Wulf."

"No. But for you and your Edwin. Life goes on."

She lay down by the fire, pulled her cloak tight round her and was warmed by her memories.

Runaway Victories

The Normans won at Hastings because they ran away and the Saxons left their strong position to chase after them.

It was reported that this happened a second time when the right-hand side of the Norman army seemed to retreat then turned round to beat the Saxons on level ground. But the second time this happened the retreat was probably deliberate. It was part of the battle-plan (or "tactics"). It wasn't the first time – or the last time – that tricks were used to fool the enemy.

The Greeks tried for ten years to capture the city of Troy and only succeeded when they pretended to run away, leaving behind their wooden horse.

Tricks such as these have been used all over the world, hundreds of times, and yet armies still fall for them and end up being defeated. Perhaps they should read their history books! Here are a few examples…

1. In AD 1241 Sun Pin was a Chinese General who couldn't get his enemy, P'ang Chuan, to fight a battle. Sun Pin crossed into P'ang's country and ordered his men to light 100,000 camp-fires the first night. The next night he ordered that just 50,000 should be lit, and 20,000 the third night. P'ang's spies reported this and when Sun Pin turned his army round and marched away, P'ang was sure the enemy forces were running back home. He chased after them. When he reached a narrow pass at nightfall he saw a tree stripped of its bark with a

F
A
C
T

F
I
L
E

message written on it. "Strike a light!" he called to his attendants. A torch flared into life and P'ang read the words: "Under this tree P'ang Chuan shall die." As P'ang read the last word his body was riddled with arrows from Sun Pin's archers.

2. In AD 685 King Ecgfrith ruled northern England and was tired of attacks from the Picts who came down from Scotland. He gathered a powerful army and headed north – but couldn't find a Pict army to defeat. He marched deeper and deeper into enemy land and still they fled in front of him. Then he was given a message that the Picts were in the next valley. All he had to do was climb through Nechtan Pass and defeat them. Nechtan Pass was narrow and his men had to walk in single file. A single boulder stopped the whole army and men bumped into one another in the mist. That's when the Picts came screaming out from behind their rocky hiding-places. They cut Ecgfrith and his army to pieces. Only one English man survived to tell the tale.

3. In the 1130s King Stephen attacked Harptree Castle in England, but the defenders were safe behind strong walls and had plenty of food. He could have waited a year and failed to take the castle. So he packed his tents and marched away. The castle defenders decided to chase after him and attack the back of the marching column. The Harptree soldiers hurried down the road but couldn't find Stephen's army. When they went home, tired and dusty, they found him soon enough. He had gone round in a wide circle and came back to find Harptree Castle undefended!

4. In 1346 the Scottish army faced a small English army on a hilltop at Neville's Cross, Durham. They marched in to attack – and were given a nasty shock. There was a much larger army waiting for them just over the hill. By then it was too late to go back and they had fallen into the trap. The Scottish commander who led the front-line troops saw the size of the English army and offered to lead the troops at the back instead! It didn't do him any good. The Scots were massacred and the street leading to the battlefield is still known as Redhills, because of the blood that once flowed there.

5. Two hundred years later at Solway Moss (1542) a Scottish army of 20,000 men came up against an English army of 3,000 on a hilltop. They weren't going to fall for the same trick again. The Scots didn't attack; they waited. The little English army moved forward – the Scots took a few steps back and panicked. The steps backwards became a stampede; they had a swamp behind them and thousands were drowned, hundreds captured and the rest fled. But the English 3,000 were exactly that. There was no one else on the other side of the hill.

6. If you want to set a trap for an enemy then you have to offer some "bait" in the trap. In the 1840s the British Army was trying to fight in Afghanistan and failing miserably. But the old "runaway" tactic still worked for them. The upper-class soldiers fought on horses, the poor soldiers fought on foot. When they needed men to tempt the Afghan fighters to chase them you can imagine who got the job – the poor foot-soldiers. The horse-soldiers went into hiding while the foot-soldiers had to march on to the plain and fire a few shots at the Afghans. When the Afghans started to charge the foot-soldiers had to run away. The horse-soldiers came out of their hiding place and attacked; a witness said "the slaughter was tremendous". The foot-soldiers had risked their lives – the horse-soldiers got the medals!

F
A
C
T

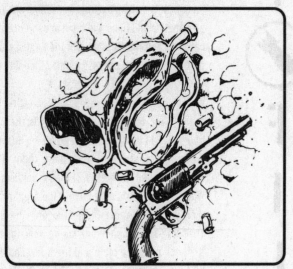

F
I
L
E

7. In 1866 the native American Indians used the idea of pretending to run away. A US Cavalry officer called William Fetterman hated the Sioux Indians and boasted, "Give me eighty men and I'll march through the whole Sioux nation." Strangely enough, he had exactly 80 men when he set off to guard a group of wood-cutters on 21 December 1866. His commander had told him, "If the Sioux attack, don't chase them past Lodge Trail Ridge". A small group of Sioux attacked and Fetterman chased after them – just as he'd been told *not* to. As they crossed Lodge Trail Ridge they discovered 2,000 warriors were waiting for them. All 80 Cavalry men died in the trap. Bugler Adolph Metzger was probably the last to die, using his bugle as a weapon till it was battered shapeless.

8. You don't have to use live soldiers to fool the enemy. In 1944 the British and US forces wanted to invade Europe and land in Normandy. They wanted the German enemy to think they would land at Calais. So they took a corpse, dressed it as

F

A

C

T

F

I

L

E

a senior British officer and left it floating in the sea where the Germans would find it. The body had a briefcase full of invasion plans – plans to land in Calais. The Germans believed this lie and their best troops were in the wrong place when the invasion forces landed.

MASSACRED

Reports of battles can be boring lists of names and numbers of the dead and wounded. But we are lucky that some reporters have told us the interesting happenings – the ones that show the courage and the stupidity, the cruelty and the cowardice, the strength of some characters and the weakness of others. The Battle of Crécy had them all and we are lucky enough to have the wonderful report of the battle written by the French writer, Jean (John) Froissart. He lived through one of most dramatic battles of the Hundred Years' War.

The 15,000 English were led by King Edward III and his son, the 15-year-old Edward Prince of Wales, later known as the Black Prince. They had 4,000 knights who fought on foot and 11,000 archers armed with quick-firing longbows. The 40,000 French were led by King Philip VI and had 12,000 knights on horseback with 6,000 archers from Genoa, who used powerful but slow crossbows.

Date: 26 August 1376
Place: Crécy, northern France
The girl sat on the crest of the hill and looked down towards the village below. The houses were thatched and white-washed. The

small fields were like a patchwork quilt of yellow corn stubble, green grazing grass dotted with sheep and cattle, and the rich browns of ploughed soil. To her left a lazy river trickled through swamp patches of a brilliant green.

"It's peaceful," she said.

The man walked up to her and rested his hand on her shoulder. He wore a leather jerkin over a cream woollen shirt and grey trousers. "What's the date today, girl?" he asked.

"August the 26th, Uncle," she replied.

"And the time?"

The girl squinted up at the sky. The sun was long past its highest point and moving towards the purple plains and the haze over the sea to the west. "About six hours after noon, Uncle John. Maybe three hours before nightfall."

"Then it is exactly 30 years ago to the hour that the battle began," John Froissart said. His face was weathered to a deep shade of brown with the hours he spent travelling the dangerous roads. His dark eyes burned fiercely under his heavy eyebrows.

"The massacre?" the girl asked.

"Oh, it was to be a massacre all right, Marie. The little English army was waiting over there with their backs to the sun," her uncle said, pointing across the shallow valley to the far hillside. "The English were waiting to be massacred by the largest force of knights the world had ever seen. French knights in armour who would ride down from here and cut the English to pieces. That was the plan."

"But it's late to be starting a battle," young Marie argued.

The man gave a grim smile. His brother's daughter was clever and interested. His own sons had never wanted to visit the old battlefield. "King Philip of France said it was too late," he told her. "He ordered his army to make camp. They ignored him."

"But he was king!" the girl protested.

"There were three *other* kings in that army, and knights from Germany, Bohemia and Spain too. They weren't going to take orders from a king of France. They were thirsting for English blood. These roads were packed with local peasants as well as soldiers. And the peasants were chanting, 'Kill! Kill! Kill! Kill the Goddans!'"

"Why did they call the English 'Goddans', Uncle John?"

"Because the English were terrible men for swearing. They went around saying, 'God damn this and God damn that'. The French called them Goddans because that's all the English seemed to say! Anyway, I was telling you about the battle."

The girl knelt on the turf and smoothed her pale blue dress. "Sorry, Uncle John. So where did the knights charge?"

"Let me tell this in my own way, girl! The knights didn't charge straight away. At least King Philip made his voice heard *that* time. The English were on that far hillside in three rows. Their archers with longbows at the front, their knights standing behind them, and the men at arms with long, sharp axes called pikes at the back."

The girl half closed her eyes and tried to picture it. "Why weren't the English knights on their horses?" she asked.

"Because they had dug holes in the ground in front of their archers. Horse traps that a charging knight would fall into. They had been there since the night before and were ready for the French attack. The English knights were simply waiting. The French had been marching all day and they were tired, especially their bowmen. They'd had to carry their heavy crossbows and bolts and they arrived here complaining of being exhausted."

"I would too," Marie muttered.

"But once King Philip saw the attack was going ahead he sent six thousand of the bowmen forward. The trouble was their heavy wooden shields were on the carts at the back of the army. They had to fire a bolt then take almost a minute to load it again. You see their problem?"

The girl nodded. "While they were reloading they had no shelter from the English bowmen."

"Exactly! And then they had terrible bad luck. There was a heavy downpour of rain. It soaked the strings of the crossbows and made them weak. They couldn't fire half as far."

"But it was the same for the English," Marie said.

"It wasn't!" the man cried and he walked across to sit next to her. "The English were using simple longbows. When the rain fell they just took off the strings, rolled them up and put them in their pockets. Then the rain stopped. The sun came out again. See? Just like today. Low in the sky and right in the eyes of the French. The French crossbows fired blindly into the sun – and with their wet bowstrings the bolts fell short."

The man looked up into the sky where some birds circled lazily in the evening air. "A flock of crows flew between the two armies and darkened the sky for a minute. The peasants said that was a bad sign. And as the sky cleared of crows it was filled with arrows. The English archers stepped forward and started firing back. It was like a storm of steel-tipped arrows falling on the French archers. No one had ever seen such a terrible force before. Of course the French turned and tried to escape."

"Who could blame them?"

"The French knights could blame them! They saw their crossbowmen flocking back towards them and became really angry. The knights moved forward and cut their way through the French bowmen to get at the English!"

"The French knights killed the French archers?" the girl said frowning. "That's mad."

"King Philip gave the order himself!" the man cried. "'Kill the foot-soldiers! Kill the foot-soldiers!' he ordered. 'They are getting in our way!' Of course the bowmen didn't stand there waiting to be killed. They fought back. And all the time the English arrows poured down. Then at last the French knights were clear to charge the English over there. You see the windmill at the top of the far hill?"

The girl squinted into the low sun. "Yes, Uncle."

"The English king, Edward III, stood there and watched the battle. He sent his son, the Black Prince, to fight with the knights while he sat watching."

"The coward," Marie said.

"The king said it was time the boy won his own fame as a fighter. After all, the lad was fifteen."

"Not much older than me," Marie said. "Did they kill him?"

"The French knights swept across the valley here and towards the English knights standing, waiting for them. Many of them stumbled in the traps the English had dug. Others were shot down with English arrows. But some French and German knights broke through and reached the Black Prince."

"But did they kill him?" she demanded.

"The Earl of Warwick hurried to warn King Edward who was watching from a spot near that windmill. 'Sir, your son is attacked by the French. His generals are asking that you send help. If more French arrive then he will be in great danger!' The king replied, 'Is my son dead? Has he fallen off his horse? Is he too badly wounded to help himself?' The knight said he was alive and fighting. So King Edward said, 'Go back, Sir Thomas, and tell those who sent you not to send for me again today. And tell them not to expect help from me so long as my son is alive. I order them to let my son win his spurs. I am determined that all the glory and honour of the day shall be given to him alone.'"

"Would you do that with your sons, Uncle John?" the girl asked.

He shook his head slowly. "King Edward of England was a harder man than me. I suppose that's why he won battles!"

"But he didn't win this one, did he? The English were massacred, weren't they?"

"A lot of men died here, Marie. Even the valiant King Charles of Bohemia was among the dead."

"Why was he valiant?"

"Because he was blind, Marie. Blind as the stones on the ground. Yet he turned to his knights and said, 'I ask you to lead me far into the battle that I may strike at least one stroke with my sword.' The knights agreed and so that they wouldn't lose him in the crowd they fastened the reins of all their horses together. They put the king at their head so he could have his wish. Then they advanced towards the English. The next day they were found dead on the ground with their horses all tied together."

"But when did they massacre the Goddans, Uncle John?"

The man frowned but didn't answer her question. Instead he went on, "By ten o'clock the king of France had no more than sixty knights to defend him. His friends said, 'Your Majesty, you have to retreat while you have the chance and take no more risks.

You may have lost this battle but you can always win the next one.'"

"He ran away?"

"He had no choice. They took the bridle off the king's horse and dragged him off the battlefield. Then came the worst part of the battle. French knights wandered up and down the battlefield in the darkness, attacking the English in small parties. The English destroyed them easily. The Goddans had decided to spare no one and to take no prisoners. That evening, after the battle, the English stayed on the battlefield and did not leave it to pursue anyone. They guarded their position and defended themselves against anyone who attacked them. When the English heard no more shouting from their enemies, they knew they had won. They made great fires and lighted torches. King Edward came down from his viewpoint at the windmill. He hadn't needed to put on his helmet and fight that day. He advanced towards the Prince of Wales and kissed him. He said. 'Sweet son, God give you strength. You are truly my son and have behaved heroically today. You are worthy to become king when I die.'"

"How do you know all this, Uncle John?"

"Because I make it my work to talk to people who were there. I've been to England and Germany and Spain, always asking questions. I write down everything they tell me."

"Why?"

"Because some things are so important they should never be forgotten."

"Like the Black Prince?"

"And like foolish, brave old Charles of Bohemia."

"He was the bravest of them all," Marie said.

"Was he? Remember those fifteen thousand English facing a mighty forty thousand enemies. If you were English you may think every one of those fifteen thousand were heroes," her Uncle John explained.

"But what about the massacre, Uncle John? You said you'd tell me."

He took a deep breath. "The battle finished around midnight. When the sun rose the next morning the French had gone. The English went out on to the battlefield and looked for their dead and wounded friends. There were hardly any. But the ground was thick with dead French knights and soldiers. It was a massacre, Marie. But it was a massacre of the greatest French knights in all their glittering armour by English peasants with simple wooden bows."

"And did the Black Prince become king?" the girl asked.

"No. He died of a fever two months ago, they say."

"The English still want to take our land, Uncle John. When I'm older I'm going to buy a sword and a horse and I'm going to drive them out of France!"

The man stood up and for the first time that afternoon he laughed. He helped his niece to her feet. "No, Marie, a woman can't fight for France. You'll have to wait for the men to finish this war."

"Hah!" she snorted. "Then we'll have to wait a hundred years!"

John Froissart died in 1410. Just two years later a girl called Joan was born. She led the French to some great victories over the English. In time the English captured her and burned her at the stake. But the woman warrior had broken the English power in France and they never recovered.

The war ended in 1453, 116 years after it had started. After the loss of thousands of lives and great devastation the English had achieved nothing – except some glorious memories of victories like Crécy. Victories recorded by a devoted French historian, John Froissart.

Longbows, Crossbows, Swords and Pikes

1. Throughout the history of war there have been battles won by the clever use of weapons. The English longbow won the Battle of Crécy. Before then everyone had feared the crossbow. The bolts from the crossbow could punch through a knight's armour and this worried many people. It meant that a peasant with a crossbow could kill a knight in armour – that was totally against the knights' idea of war! Peasants were not supposed to kill knights!

2. A knight was a Christian who was not looking to kill an enemy the way a frightened peasant would. The knight's aim was to capture his enemy and hold him for ransom. That way the knight would win money but, more importantly, win honour.

3. Church leaders tried to pass a law that would ban the crossbow. Their efforts failed. But the crossbow was not a perfect weapon. It was heavy (around 10 kilos) and took time to reload. The crossbowman had to shelter behind a large shield while he attached a winding device and fitted a new bolt. Even the best crossbowman could fire no more than three bolts a minute. And the crossbowmen at Crécy had left their shields behind in the long march! No wonder they turned back under the hail of English arrows.

4. The longbow used by the English was light and the string could be rolled up and put in the pocket to protect it from the rain storm that began the battle. It could fire over 250 metres and an archer could send 12 to 15 arrows a minute into the enemy soldiers. The points of the arrows were stuck in the ground so they could be snatched up quickly. But this dirty point had the extra advantage of giving a wounded enemy blood poisoning.

5. The English bowmen also carried swords so they could fight as foot-soldiers when their supply of arrows ran out. They would be fighting for their lives. Enemy knights would not bother ransoming an archer — he would kill every archer he could find. Enemy foot- soldiers had a particularly nasty punishment for English archers who were taken alive — they would cut off two fingers of the right hand to stop the archer ever using a bow again.

6. The most fearsome men in the English army were the Welsh pike men. They had a long cutlass attached to the end of a pike. During a battle they had the gruesome job of finishing off the enemy wounded. They went from body to body looking for a chink in the armour and sliding the cutlass in.

F A C T F I L E

7. For 200 years after Crécy the longbow ruled the battlefields of Europe. In time, of course, the bows were replaced by guns. But there is a curious story that cannon were first used in a battle ... at Crécy! While the longbow was showing itself to be the best weapon in the world, its replacement was already waiting in the wings. Froissart didn't mention cannon at Crécy, but an Italian called Villani reported, "The fire of the cannon made so much noise that it seemed as if God himself was thundering." Strangely Villani was in prison in Florence at the time of the battle so he can't have seen the cannon for himself.

8. King Edward III had cannon fired by gunpowder in London, but it's doubtful if he'd have taken them on his long march through France. Cannon-balls found at the battlefield in 1850 were made of cast iron — and cast iron cannon-balls weren't invented until 100 years later. It's a mystery.

CAPTURED

Two thousand years ago a Roman poet said, "It is sweet and good to die for your country". That idea of fighting and dying for a country has driven a lot of people to fight very bravely in a lot of wars. That sort of courage has created "heroes" and "heroines". Dead heroes are loved and respected. The really sad cases can be the heroes who don't die in battle! Heroes like John Paul Jones of the United States...

Date: 18 July 1792
Place: Paris, France

The room smelled of stale cabbage and dead cats. The heat was suffocating. It was dark, with just a little of the brilliant Paris sunshine spilling through the broken shutters.

The bed was no more than a straw-filled mattress on the floor. The man in the patched nightshirt lay on the bed with the blankets thrown off. He hadn't shaved for weeks and his thin, brown hair and beard were tangled and matted. His pale watery eyes looked up at the young woman dressed in black. "I've no money for rent," he said. "But I am going to be made the American Ambassador to Algeria soon. Any day now. Any day. I will be able to pay you twice over."

The woman snorted softly. "And they are going to make me queen of France."

"You are making fun of me," the man said. Sweat was running into his eyes and his breathing was shallow and fast.

"Why not? This is revolution," she cried. "You heard that the mob attacked the royal family in their palace, did you? King Louis and his evil Marie Antoinette will be executed. Then we will all be free and equal. Why shouldn't I become queen?"

"I know all about revolution," the man sighed. "I fought for the Americans to free them from the British."

She sniffed and looked down at his thin body in the filthy nightshirt. "You were a fighter?"

"A hero," he said.

"American?"

"Yes."

"But you do not speak like an American," she argued.

"No," he agreed. "I was born in Scotland."

"Then you are British," she said simply. "When will I get my rent?"

Before he could answer there was a tap at the door and a man in a dark suit, a fine grey wig and a fresh white cravat entered the room. "Mr Jones?" he asked. "You sent for me? I am Doctor Marleau."

The woman turned her thin face to the visitor and said to the doctor, "He will offer to pay you next week. Next week he will become American Ambassador to Algeria."

The doctor shrugged. "We call it delirium. In a fever men may imagine all sorts." He sat next to the sick man and lifted his wrist to feel his pulse. He shook his head. "You have pain?"

"My head aches – and my lungs."

The doctor rested his head against the sick man's chest and listened to the rattle of his breathing. "I can give you something to make you sleep," he said. He took a small green bottle from his pocket, held it to the lips of the sick man and tipped a few drops in.

"But I will be well in time to take up my post in Algeria, won't I?" the man asked.

"It would not be wise to leave your bed just now," the doctor said.

"He'll be leaving it wrapped in a burial sheet," the woman muttered.

The doctor gave her a frown and shook his head. He rose and spoke close to her ear. "At least make his last hours content," he said. "We can at least do that."

The woman lowered her head a little in shame. "Of course," she murmured. Then she raised her voice. "Now, Doctor, Mr Jones was telling me that he was a hero of the American Revolution," she said brightly.

The doctor sat on a bench at the door and smiled, "Is that so, Mr Jones?"

"The truth is my name is really John Paul. I had to change it," the sick man said.

"Why was that, Mr Jones?"

"When I was twenty-five years old I was captain of the trading ship *Betsy*. We'd load a cargo in Britain and sail to Tobago. When we got there we'd sell the cargo and use the money to buy sugar and tobacco and cocoa and rum. When we got back to Britain we'd sell it for a great profit. Why, I was a rich man by the time I was twenty-five. I thought of buying my own tobacco plantation in America. I was worth at least £2,500!"

"Then you should be able to pay the rent," the woman muttered sourly.

"But in 1774 I had the greatest misfortune of my life. Some of the crew said they didn't want to put their share of the money

60

into a new cargo in Tobago. They wanted the cash. One of the men seemed to be the ringleader and he came after me with a club. I ran to my cabin – they thought I was running away. But a Scotsman doesn't run from a fight. I went to fetch my sword. Oh, but he was a tough fighter that one. I wanted to wound him in the arm. Make him drop his club. But he drove me back towards one of the hatches on the deck. One more step and I'd have crashed twenty feet to the bottom of the ship. I lashed out desperately!"

"You hit him?" the doctor asked.

"I killed him!"

"It was self-defence," the doctor shrugged.

"We were in Tobago," John Paul Jones sighed. "The man was from Tobago. I would never have had a fair trial. I changed my name from John Paul to John Paul Jones and left the *Betsy*. Of course I had to leave my fortune too. I went to America to live with my brother in Virginia."

"You were what they call an outlaw," the doctor nodded.

"I was. But we Scots are used to being persecuted. By the time I reached America they were trying to break free from British rule but it was hard. The British ruled the Atlantic Ocean, you see? The British had a hundred fighting ships – the Americans had just five armed merchant ships! I tell you, David had a better chance against Goliath."

"But David won," the doctor said with a smile.

"Exactly!" the man replied and there was a rattle in his throat that could have been a chuckle. "I joined the warship *Alfred* as a lieutenant and sailed against the British. Now, we didn't want to be hanged as pirates if we were captured so we had to have a proper American flag for our ships."

61

"You have your stars and stripes flag," the doctor said.

"Ah, but in 1775 we had nothing. So I came up with the idea of thirteen red and white stripes – one stripe for every colony!"

The woman took a deep breath and raised her eyebrows. "He is not only the American Ambassador to Algeria but he is now the man who invented the American flag! This delirium is bad, doctor."

The doctor waved a hand to quieten her. "So your five little ships sailed against the mighty British navy and David beat Goliath?"

The sick man's clouded eyes cleared for a moment and he focused them on the man in the dark suit. "War isn't like that, Doctor. David sailed against Goliath and Goliath blew him out of the water!" He gave a chuckle then stopped suddenly as a sharp pain stabbed his chest. "We raided a British post on the Bahamas to steal gunpowder. But on the way back we ran into one British warship, HMS *Glasgow*. We didn't have any plan of attack. Our five ships went in one at a time – and the British picked us off one at a time. It was a shambles. Ten of our men were killed to just one British sailor. A disaster."

"So you needed more ships," the doctor said.

"No! We needed to fight in a different way with the ships we had. They made me skipper of a twelve-gun sloop, *Providence*, and my orders were to roam the sea attacking British traders and fishing boats. We couldn't beat their navy but we could make their trade suffer. We knew the British would hate that."

"I remember the French navy supported you, Monsieur Jones. The British have never forgiven the French. I think we will have to go to war with them again soon."

"Then let me tell you, the way to beat them is to *attack*. I took my ship all the way across the Atlantic and attacked the British navy where it would least expect it. In its own ports. Can't you see what a wonderful plan it was? We couldn't beat their navy in the open waters of the Atlantic. But if we crept into one of their harbours at night we could set fire to their ships and do more damage than the rest of our navy could do in a year!"

"You went to Portsmouth?"

"No. I started my sailing off the south-west coast of Scotland. I knew the English port of Whitehaven well. I took my ship to Whitehaven and went ashore to spike their cannon so the rest of my crew could set fire to their ships in the docks." The sick man's face was glowing with sweat and his breath was coming faster now. The doctor placed a hand on his shoulder and pushed him gently back on to the bed.

"A daring idea," Doctor Marleau said gently.

"Ah, but the men wanted the safer job of attacking merchant ships and robbing them. They were little better than pirates, Doctor. Pirates."

"So you never attacked Whitehaven?"

"We did, but it was a sad joke. My crew went ashore to set fire to the boats while I spiked the guns. But what did that rabble of a crew do? They went into the Whitehaven taverns and got drunk. And when they were drunk they told everyone what they were planning to do! The sentries almost caught us while we were trying to set fire to a ship and I only just escaped with my life."

"You burned nothing, then?"

"Two ships. But then my candles went out," he sighed.

John Paul Jones closed his eyes. The woman widened her nostrils in disgust. "Now he *is* dreaming."

The man on the bed kept his eyes closed and went on with his story. "The British had arrested a lot of American sailors but they didn't treat them like prisoners of war. They treated them like common criminals and shut them away in filthy floating prisons they call 'hulks'. I decided it was time to set them free. I thought that if I captured an important British lord then I could trade him for my American comrades."

"Why not capture King George himself?" the woman sneered.

"I knew the area around Saint Mary's Isle where I'd been brought up. I knew I could capture the Earl of Selkirk in his home. And the men would be happy because they could have any treasure they found in his house. I drew them a plan of the house and the doors and where to find the Earl's room. It was a perfect plan!"

The doctor leaned forward. "And it worked."

The Scotsman on the bed sighed. "No, the Earl wasn't at home when they attacked. They came back with just a few silver candlesticks. I bought the candlesticks myself and sent them back to the house I was so ashamed."

"I thought you said you were a success against the British," the doctor said quietly. "You were going to tell me how the French can beat them. You have just described failure!"

"Ah, yes," Jones said and his voice was weaker now. "On the way home from Saint Mary's Isle we met a British sloop about our own size – HMS *Drake* – and we beat her. She surrendered and we got two-hundred and twenty-eight American prisoners in exchange for British sailors we'd captured. I was an American hero! They wrote songs about me and my ship! We weren't treated as pirates after that. We were a navy, and the British were afraid of us."

"The man who hits and runs is hard to defend against," the doctor agreed. "You never know where he will strike next!"

"I could have done so much with a faster ship. The Americans gave me an old French tub, *Bonhomme Richard,* to sail in and I still beat the British. We met their HMS *Serapis* off the coast of Yorkshire and I ran up the stars and stripes flag. Of course they pounded us with their cannon. Blew up two of my eighteen-pound cannon in the first minutes."

"You couldn't hope to beat a British warship," the doctor said.

"Not with fire power. But I could if I could get close enough to board her. *Serapis* was trying to escape but I was a better sailor. I caught her and grappled our *Bonhomme Richard* to her. My muskets could fire down on her decks and kill their gunners. But where their gunners survived they were pounding our old ship out of the water. Round after round of cannon shot they smashed into us. At one point my chief gunner cried, 'For God's sake, mercy!' The captain of *Serapis* called back, 'Do you cry for mercy?' but I told him, 'We haven't even begun to fight yet!'"

John Paul Jones gave a painful, hollow cough that left him twisted in agony and panting. "We haven't even begun to fight yet!" he gasped. "That's what my boys remembered. Those are the words that they took back to America."

"You won?"

"In the end. After two hours," John Paul Jones whispered and his voice was weak now. "The British captain surrendered. We boarded *Serapis*. *Bonhomme Richard* sank the next day. We took *Serapis* back to America. Five hundred prisoners. Heroes. All heroes. Goliath beaten. Your King Louis gave me the Order of Merit."

"Louis," the woman spat. "He'll be dead soon. France doesn't want a king."

"Not dead soon. Going to be Ambassador to Algeria."

"You must rest," the doctor said.

"The Americans never gave me another ship. The Americans got their independence and sold their warships. Didn't need them. Didn't need me. No use for a hero when a war's over. No need for me. Came to France. Your revolution started. Can't get back home to America."

"But they will reward you now by making you Ambassador to Algeria," the doctor said. He covered the man on the bed with a blanket.

"He's no more Ambassador to Algeria than I am," the woman snapped. "When will I get my rent?"

"How much?"

"Ten sous."

The doctor reached into his pocket and gave her a coin. "Let him dream while he can. He has not got much longer."

"But that story..."

"It was a good story," the doctor shrugged. "Worth ten sous." He rose from the bench and walked to the door. He stepped out of the stinking roof into the stifling heat of the Paris street. A stranger in a fine cutaway coat with a satin waistcoat was trying to talk to people in the street. He caught the eye of the doctor and walked across to him. "Excuse me sir, do you speak English?"

"I do."

"I am looking for a man called John Paul Jones."

"You are American?"

"That's right. From the American Embassy. I have an urgent message for him."

The doctor looked towards the shabby house he'd just left. "You are not going to tell me he's an American hero?"

"You've heard of him, then? Yes, he's as famous in America as Washington. Invented the striped flag!"

"And you are going to tell me he is being offered the post of Ambassador to Algeria."

The man in the satin waistcoat blinked. "But ... how on earth could you possibly know that ... unless you've met John Paul Jones, of course."

The doctor wiped a trickle of sweat from his forehead. "It seems that I have met John Paul Jones," he said weakly. "It seems that I really *have* met him."

F
A
C
T

War at Sea

O
F
I
L
E

John Paul Jones died before the news of his honoured position reached him. He was buried in a pauper's grave in Paris. A hundred years later his grave was discovered and his body taken back to the United States. He was given a hero's funeral at the naval school he had done so much to create. Now there is a museum dedicated to him and he is recognized as one of the men who helped America win her independence.

It's all too late, of course. John Paul, who called himself John Paul Jones, must have died a lonely and disappointed man, feeling sure that he'd been forgotten by the nation he'd fought for.

For thousands of years war at sea has created its own heroes and heroines. Some individual names, like John Paul Jones, are remembered but most have been forgotten. Sea battles aren't marked by war memorials for obvious reasons! But some sea battles have changed the history of the world…

1. **Salamis, Greece, 480 BC.** Long before cannon were invented, ships tried to sink one another by ramming. Battles were deadly affairs because there was no room in the warships to take enemy survivors on board. If your ship lost the ramming battle then you were left to drown. At Salamis, 300 Greek ships faced 800 Persian invaders. But the channel was so narrow the Persians couldn't get all of their ships into the fight. The bronze rams on the front of the Greek ships demolished over 200 Persian ships. The Persian invasion was over and it remains the world's biggest sea battle, with 190,000 men involved. But … there is a strange story that the Greeks would have run away from the huge Persian force if a ghostly ship hadn't ordered them to turn back and fight. After the battle no one ever saw that ship again!

2. **Actium, the Gulf of Arta, 31 BC.** The Romans attacked the huge Egyptian ships of Queen Cleopatra and her lover, Mark Antony. The light Roman ships avoided the Egyptian rams and sent fire arrows into the enemy fleet. This was not a day for heroes and heroines, though. Cleopatra thought her ships were losing so she sailed off to safety and Mark Antony hurried after her, abandoning his loyal men. They soon surrendered rather than die at sea. Antony and Cleopatra killed themselves a week later.

3. **Swold Island, Vinland, AD 1000.** The Vikings fought by climbing into one another's ships and battling it out hand to hand. Viking Prince Olaf was tricked into fighting his brother-in-law, King Sweyn of Denmark, who had three times as many ships. Olaf's men were keen to row away and save themselves. Olaf was braver (or more foolish) and cried, "No men of mine ever run away. The gods can take my life but I'll never take flight." Unfortunately the gods took the lives of all his men as well. When all was lost, Olaf jumped into the sea, held his shield above his head, and sank.

F
A
C
T

F
I
L
E

4. **The English Channel, near Sluys, 1340.** The French ships set out to stop King Edward III's invasion and took the unusual step of chaining their ships together. The English were able to move freely among the chained mass and wreck the French defence. But, strangest of all was the fact that the entire crew of one English ship was killed by men throwing *rocks* from the forecastle of a French ship.

5. **England, 1588.** The Spanish king Philip sent 130 ships and 30,000 men to pick up a Spanish army in the Netherlands and invade England. The huge force of mighty galleons was known as the Armada and should have swept the smaller English ships out of their way. There is a famous story that one of the English commanders, Francis Drake, was playing bowls when the Armada was sighted. He said he'd finish his game of bowls first: "There's time for that and time to beat the Spaniards after." The English sent fire-ships among the Spanish galleons at night. They panicked and lost ships and men. Storms in the English Channel finished off many more and the Spanish invasion plan was in ruins. Amazingly the Spanish gunners fired 100,000 cannon-balls without scoring a single hit!

6. **West Indies, 1731.** English captain Robert Jenkins was a peaceful trader in the West Indies when he was arrested by Spanish coastguards who cut off his ear. Jenkins sent the ear, in a case, to his king to demand revenge. It was seven years before the British took revenge; the ear was passed around parliament and the angry MPs decided it was one more reason to go to war with Spain – which they did in 1739. It became known as the War of Jenkins' Ear.

7. **The American Revolution, 1775-76.** Before John Paul Jones won his famous victory over the *Serapis*, the Americans had a curious victory over a British schooner, the *Margaretta*. The British crew had anchored in Machias Bay and gone to church. There they were attacked by farmers waving sickles. The British jumped out of their seats and raced back to their ship. Two boatloads of angry Americans followed them, climbed aboard the *Margaretta* and killed the captain. The crew surrendered. A year later in 1776, the British warship *Eagle* was also at anchor when it was the victim of another unusual American attack. It was the first ship to be attacked by a submarine. The little underwater attacker was invented by an American farmer and called *American Turtle*. It looked like a two-metre, wooden egg and carried a barrel of gunpowder outside, which was timed to explode soon after it was released under an enemy ship. The torpedo failed to sink the *Eagle* but the sight of it terrified a crew of sailors who chased after the submarine. It eventually escaped to safety.

8. **Cape Trafalgar, 1805.** The French leader, Napoleon Bonaparte, decided to invade England just as William the Conqueror had 739 years before to the week. But this time he had to get past a British fleet first. It was commanded by the one-eyed, one-armed Admiral Lord Horatio Nelson. As the French came in sight Nelson signalled to his fleet, "England expects that every man will do his duty". And every man did. Unfortunately Nelson was shot by a French sniper. As he lay dying his officers told him that they had destroyed 18 of the 33 French and Spanish enemy ships. Nelson replied, "I'd reckoned on 20". Then he said, "Thank God I have done my duty," and he died. He is one sea hero who has not been forgotten. His statue stands on a tall column in Trafalgar Square (named after the

F
A
C
T
F
I
L
E

battle) in London. After one of his victories a woman asked, "I want to change the name of my pub from the King's Arms to The Nelson Arms. Is that all right?" He replied, "Don't be ridiculous — I only have one".

POUNDED

For thousands of years soldiers have gone into battle on horseback. Horses carried them to battle, were stabbed and whipped and shot and killed – and never seemed to complain. But it is good to know that not all horses were so ready to stand and be butchered by a human who was not even their enemy. At least one horse believed in fighting back. Her name was Lisette and her owner, Baron de Marbot, told the remarkable story of her fight for France...

Date: February 1807
Place: Eylau, Poland

To understand my story you have to go back to the start of it. That was in the autumn of 1805 when I was one of Napoleon's officers in the Grand Army. We were preparing for the coming battle against the Russians and collecting equipment. I already had two good horses and was looking for a third – I needed a charger. A horse that wouldn't be afraid to face the muskets, the cannon and the sabres that the Russian army would be attacking us with. I hadn't a lot of money – but I did have a piece of good luck.

I heard that a German called von Aister was offering a horse for sale – he had been my tutor at university. "These days I am the teacher of a rich Swiss banker's children," he told me when we met in the town tavern. "The master has a fine stable of horses but there's one in particular he's willing to sell. A beautiful mare called Lisette. And she's cheap."

"What's the catch?" I asked suspiciously. With horses in such short supply the price of the most ruined nag was five thousand francs. I knew that von Aister wouldn't try to trick me but I felt there was something he wasn't telling me.

"She's as light as a deer," he said. I noticed that he hadn't answered my question. "She's so well broken a child could lead her."

"But..."

"She's no more afraid of gunfire than she is of her bag of oats." He smiled but wouldn't look me in the eye.

"Professor von Aister," I said, holding up a hand to stop him. "Why is your Swiss banker selling the lovely Lisette?"

"He isn't," von Aister said. "It's his wife's horse."

I sighed and drew my sword. This action stopped all the conversation in the tavern and even the pot boys stopped to look at me. I grabbed the professor's arm by the wrist and held his hand down on the table. "Sir," I said. "Every time you fail to answer my question I will cut off one of your fingers."

His hand jumped and his fingers curled up into a fist. "You wouldn't."

"Let's find out, shall we?" I placed the edge of the sword against his knuckle. "Now, tell me. What is wrong with this horse."

"It bites," he said quickly.

I kept the sword there and went on, "What does it bite? Its hay? Or the door to its stable?"

"People."

"This horse bites people?"

75

"Yes."

"Which people?"

"People it doesn't like."

"And which people does Lisette not like?"

"All people."

I removed my sword and released his wrist. "You are saying that this horse bites anyone and everyone?"

"Yes – bites like a bulldog. But apart from that..."

"It's a wonderful horse," I nodded. "How much does the banker want for this bulldog-horse?"

"He paid five thousand francs for the horse," von Aister said.

"Then he discovered it was a biter," I smiled. "He'll sell it for less than that now, won't he?"

"He will listen to lower offers – especially now," he said in a low voice.

"Now?"

"Now that it's killed one of its grooms."

I am sure my mouth fell open at this news. I took a long drink from my glass of brandy. "How?"

"It grabbed the young man by the stomach and ripped out his bowels," von Aister said, and his face was pale and sick at the thought.

"One thousand francs," I offered. "Not a sou more."

Von Aister nodded and hurried off through the crowded tavern. I'll swear he was counting his fingers.

And that's how I came to own Lisette. A delightful, bold mare who took only five men to get a saddle on her. If you placed a blindfold over her eyes and tied her four legs then you could get a bridle over her head. Once you were on her back she was as easy to ride as a lamb.

The trouble was I was losing grooms at the rate of one a week. They suffered terribly as the victims of her teeth, and refused to work for me. I myself had only received about ten bites a day, my arms, legs and chest were badly bruised but I would have carried on. I couldn't continue to keep her if I had no grooms. That's when a cavalry-horse trainer, Francis Woirland, came to my rescue.

"Put a couple of legs of mutton in the oven to roast," he suggested, "and bring her to the kitchen door in an hour's time."

I was puzzled by his plan but I did as he said. I placed a rope around Lisette's neck and after suffering no more than four playful nips that would each have killed a calf, I led her to the kitchen. When she saw Woirland she snorted and lunged at him, teeth bared and mouth open. He swung a gloved hand from behind his back and it held the leg of mutton, steaming and sizzling from the oven.

Lisette bit into the mutton and leapt back. She gave a scream of pain as the hot meat scalded her tongue and her gums. The mutton fell to the ground. Woirland stood in front of her and she made no move to attack him. "Now you," he said. "Take my glove and lift the mutton from the oven."

I tried the mutton trick myself as Woirland led Lisette towards me and she dashed at me. Again the mutton hurt her, her eyes rolled in fear and she looked at me with a new respect.

From then on she was as tame as a lap-dog. She was the best and bravest horse a cavalry officer could have. Even the stable-lads were safe. But let her see a stranger and she was a dragon.

That was how I came to be riding her at Eylau and how she saved 100 French lives at the great battle there in 1807. The battle was going badly for the troops on the plain – they were being smashed by the mighty Russian cannon. The 14th Regiment were on a hilltop, formed into a square and defending that hill to the last man. They would not leave the hill unless the Emperor Napoleon himself ordered it.

I was riding my Lisette near the great cemetery when the order came through for the 14th to retreat. It was my task to take the message to those men but it was a dangerous and difficult journey. The Russian dragoons had attacked time and again up that hill. Time and again the 14th had shot them down. The hill was surrounded by a wall of dead men and horses. Even with the help of the men on the hill I had trouble climbing through this dreadful fortress. But at last I reached the major in charge.

"Withdraw," I cried. "It is the order of the Emperor Napoleon himself. Withdraw!"

"And where will we go?" he asked. "The rest of the army on the plain are being torn apart by the cannon. Should we go down just to die there?"

"It's the Emperor's orders," I said helplessly.

The major shrugged. "Unfortunately I couldn't reach the plain anyway. There's a Russian column just a hundred paces away."

I looked over the massed square of our French foot-soldiers and saw the Russians advancing up the hill.

The men raised their muskets and waited calmly for the order to fire. "I can see no way to save the regiment. Go back to the Emperor," the Major said. "Tell him farewell from the 14th. Tell him we died following his orders faithfully. Take the eagle standard that he gave us. We wouldn't want to see it fall into the hands of the enemy."

He held up the bronze eagle that was attached to a heavy oak pole. He saluted it one last time and his battle-torn men cried, "Long live the Emperor!"

I could see that it would be difficult to ride away with this long pole. I could leave it behind and it would be worthless to the enemy. All I had to do was snap off the bronze eagle and carry that away.

I leaned forward to separate the eagle from the pole when one of those curious twists of fate occurred. A cannon-ball struck the back peak of my hat, not an inch from my head. If I hadn't leaned forward an instant before then it would have removed my head clean from my body.

The trouble was, the hat was firmly attached to my head by a strap. The sudden blow caused my neck to snap. I seemed to be blotted out of existence yet I didn't fall from my horse. I knew that blood was flowing from my nose, my ears and even my eyes, yet I could see and hear. I could think. I knew what was happening around me, yet I could not move a muscle of my paralysed body. I couldn't move my hands or legs to guide Lisette away from the onrushing attack. So she sat there, patient as ever.

The Russians were grenadiers who were lighting their bombs soaked in spirits ready to throw. The 14th Regiment had survived for days by eating potatoes and drinking melted snow. That morning the pitiful survivors hadn't even had that. Still they fired and then tried to defend themselves with their bayonets.

The square was broken but still they fought on in small groups. One group backed up against Lisette so that their backs were covered by her body. To my amazement she stayed quite still and quiet as the men battled to save themselves. I wanted to ride away from my certain death but I was frozen and helpless. Imagine my horror as I sat there, frozen, while the Russian grenadiers pressed closer and closer.

At last some fearsome, ugly Russian drew near and tried to reach past my French comrades to run me through with his sword. He pointed me out to his men. I was the only Frenchman on a horse. They seemed to think I was the commander and that they must kill me to win this part of the battle.

The Russians kept firing at me over their comrades' heads. I could hear the bullets whistling past my ears. One of them was bound to take away the remains of my life if it hadn't been for an incident that changed the whole course of the fight.

One of the French sergeants was wounded and fell beneath Lisette's belly. He grabbed at my boot to pull himself up while a Russian lunged at him with a bayonet. The Russian missed, but kept striking at my cloak that was billowing in the wind. At last one stroke got through and I had the curious feeling of my blood flowing hot, yet with no pain from the wound. Seeing the blood the Russian made one last effort to finish me off but he stumbled over a fallen man and missed. Instead his bayonet stuck into Lisette's rear quarters.

The pain made her forget her training. Her ferocious nature was stirred again and she sprang at the man. In one bite she tore off his nose, lips, eyebrows and all the skin of his face and made him a living death's head. Then she hurled herself among the Russians, kicking and biting furiously at all the men she could reach. The Russian officer who had been ordering his men to kill me tried to grab her reins. She seized him by his belly and carried him off with ease. She galloped with him to the foot of the hill where she tore out his entrails, smashed his body under her feet and left him dying in the snow.

The Russians were left without a leader and the French survivors were able to march down the hill to safety. As for Lisette, she carried me back across the battlefield to headquarters at the cemetery of Eylau – a near lifeless passenger. In time I recovered.

How she knew where to take me, I'll never know. How she knew a Russian enemy from her French friends, I'll never know. But I do know one thing. I know that the most vicious horse that had ever ridden in the French army had saved my life.

The War Horse

Men on horseback have an advantage over men on foot. They can strike downwards at the heads of foot-soldiers, they can wear heavier armour and carry heavier weapons and they can move more quickly around the battlefield. But foot- soldiers soon discovered that a soldier on horseback was almost helpless if you killed the horse first.

Life was dangerous for a soldier but it was worse for a horse. Some stories have happier endings than others...

1. A Greek youth, Alexander, was shown a powerful horse called Bucephalus. Unfortunately it seemed too wild to ever be ridden. He offered to tame it and his father and friends laughed. Alexander turned the horse's face towards the sun because he had noticed that it was unsettled by its own shadow. Facing the sun it could not see its dancing shadow and it calmed down immediately. Alexander climbed on its back and rode it calmly till it overcame its fear. The youth grew

F
A
C
T

F
I
L
E

up to be Alexander the Great, and Bucephalus was the horse he rode when he conquered half of the known world.

2. The Mongols conquered Asia in the 1200s thanks to their ability to cross vast distances quickly on their tough ponies and attack an enemy who thought they were still hundreds of miles away. The ponies gave them their power and they valued them. They valued them so much that a pony was seen as a rich gift to offer a god. As a result a pony would be sacrificed before each battle.

3. From AD 1200 till about 1500, knights charged on horseback with lances. Add together the weight of the knight, his armour, his horse and its armour, and the tip of the lance hit an opponent with about one *ton* of weight behind it.

4. In 1519 the Aztec Indians of Mexico were invaded by a small Spanish army. The Spanish won because the Aztecs had never seen anything like a horse before. When they saw the Spanish riding into battle, the Aztecs believed they were up against unbeatable devils and ran away. When the Aztecs did succeed in killing a horse, they realized that these were simply animals. They sent bits of the horse to all the tribes to show that these devils could be defeated. After that the Spanish were careful to bury any horses that died in a fight.

5. In 1704 in Germany, a French army was driven back because its horses started dying from a mysterious horse-plague. The soldiers couldn't ride into battle and they had no animals to pull the supply wagons. They suddenly discovered how much they relied on horses for keeping them supplied with food, weapons and clothing. The only good news for the French

FACTFILE

as they walked home, beaten, was that the enemy horses caught the plague when they grazed on the pasture that the French had just left.

6. War horses were intelligent and well trained. They knew how to line up, charge in a line, turn and retreat. They practised over and over till they learned it perfectly. After the 1815 Battle of Waterloo a dozen badly wounded horses were bought by Sir Astley Cooper who hoped to cure them. After a lot of care all 12 horses were fit again and he let them loose in his park to run freely. To his amazement he watched as the war horses lined up, shoulder to shoulder, charged forward together, turned and ran back – all without a single rider in sight. The horses seemed to enjoy this exercise first thing in the morning and people came from miles around to watch the spectacle.

7. The leader of the British troops at the Battle of Waterloo was the Duke of Wellington. He rode his horse, Copenhagen, throughout the battle – a total of 17 hours with hardly a break, often under fire from cannon and muskets. Wellington and Copenhagen survived everything … but only just. When the Duke finally climbed down from the horse's back, Copenhagen gave a lively kick of his heels and nearly brained his rider! The Duke forgave him and when the horse died over 20 years after the battle he was buried in a military grave like a heroic soldier. The headstone says that Copenhagen was ridden at Waterloo and, "Should share the glory of that glorious day."

8. Horses were still being ridden into battle in World War I, but in time they were replaced by tanks and troop carriers. However, horses have always had one advantage over tanks. In

F
A
C
T

F
I
L
E

World War II a British Officer fighting in Albania became very attached to his horse, which he called Freddy. When he left Albania he handed Freddy over to his replacement. He reached home safely and sent a message back to Albania; it said, "How is Freddy?" The next day, back came the sad reply: "Have eaten him". You can't eat a tank.

SHOT

If you have to kill your enemy then it helps if you hate him or her. But sometimes it's hard to hate another human being. Especially when you realize that, underneath the uniform, they're a lot like you...

Date: 25 December 1914
Place: Northern France

Albert Watson stamped his feet and blew on his hands. "They said this war would be over by Christmas. They say a million men have rushed to join the British Army and they're all worried that the war will finish before they get here!"

Albert was tall and too thin. His khaki uniform fitted badly; the jacket was too baggy and the tight puttee bandages round his legs made them look thin enough to snap. The young man's large boots and frost-red nose made him look like a sad, brown clown.

He looked down at Charlie Embleton, an older man with cropped hair that showed grey where he'd pushed his cap back. Charlie sat at the entrance to a crude cave dug into the frozen soil and tried to boil a kettle over a small fire in a biscuit tin. "Tell you what, Albert," he said, wiping a dew-drop off the end of his battered nose. "We'll try to keep it going a bit longer, shall we?"

"You can," Albert said. "I'm due a bit of leave. I want to get back home and see me mam! I've never had a Christmas away from home before."

"When you've been in the army as long as I have..." Charlie said solemnly.

"Here we go," Albert muttered into his hands as he cupped them and breathed on them.

"When you've been in the army as long as I have you'll forget what a Christmas at home is like!" he declared.

"Well, it's warmer than it is here, I can tell you," the younger man sniffed.

"Warmer! You don't want it any warmer, son! The cold freezes the ground nice and hard and keeps us dry in the trenches. If it wasn't for the cold we'd be over our ankles in mud."

"You always look on the bright side, don't you, Charlie?"

"You have to, son. It could be worse. We could have had orders to attack the German trenches today. Some German sniper could have sent you a little lead present from the end of his rifle. You could be lying out there in No Man's Land with a bullet in your brain," the older man told him. "Though you'd probably be safe, Albert. Your brain being such a small target and all!"

"Hah! Hah! Very amusing, Charlie."

"And you've got your chocolate and your tobacco and your Christmas card from the king and queen, haven't you?"

The young man slid a hand into the pocket of his great coat. The card was there. It made him proud to have that message from the king, even if it was just a print of His Majesty's handwriting. "May God protect you and bring you home safe." He'd read the words a hundred times until now it was too dark to read them any more. "Bring you home safe," he thought. Those four words were the ones that made him just a little homesick.

"It's quiet, isn't it?" he said suddenly. "Do you reckon Jerry's gone home for Christmas? I haven't heard a shot for hours."

But Charlie was leaning forward, his putty-face pale and frozen in the faint moonlight. Then his hand slid down to the frozen ground and wrapped itself round the rifle that lay there. "What's that noise?" he whispered.

Albert raised his head and looked across No Man's Land towards the German trenches. Charlie jumped forward and dragged the young man roughly down. "You want to get your head blown off, young Albert?" he hissed. "There's marksmen just waiting for idiots like you to look over the top!"

"You hurt my elbow!" Albert complained.

"Shush! Listen!"

The two men huddled on the frozen floor of the trench and strained their ears. "It's a band!" the young soldier breathed. "It's a blooming brass band!"

"Maybe they're going to attack us with trombones!" his mate

chuckled.

"No! They're playing 'Silent Night'!"

"A bit risky that!"

"Why?"

"It's giving away their position," the older man explained.

"Nah. But it's lovely," Albert said. His throat was tight and his eyes pricked with tears.

There was a faint whistle over the top of the music. The men clutched their heads and shrunk down, not knowing where the shell would land. It grew louder until it was a wail that drowned the music and it ended with a sudden crash that came from the far side of No Man's Land. "I told you," Charlie said. "Direct hit!"

The men rose to their feet and peered over the rim of their trench. A spiral of blue smoke climbed into the sky as echoes of the explosion faded into the evening sky.

"What they do that for?" Albert groaned. "That was nice that was!"

"That'll be the generals for you."

"Don't they know it's Christmas?"

"Christmas? They can't even spell the word."

Albert nodded sadly. "I had the same trouble spelling when I was at school."

The men turned back to their tea. It tasted terrible but it warmed them. An officer crunched through the iced mud of the trench and asked, "Everything all right, Corporal Embleton?"

Charlie scrambled to his feet, snapped a firm salute and straightened his back, "Yes, Lieutenant Armstrong."

"Shouldn't one of you be looking out? There could be Germans heading this way right at this moment!"

"Sir!" Charlie said and looked over the rim. "Cor, stone the crows!" he gasped. "Look at that!"

Albert and the officer joined him and looked across about a hundred paces. In the still evening air about 100 candles were flickering on a dozen fir trees that the Germans had raised above the trenches and planted in their half of No Man's Land. Around each tree there were groups of five to ten German soldiers, sitting and talking. In the still evening air their voices drifted across.

Then Albert called, "Merry Christmas, Fritz!"

There was a short pause and a German voice replied, "Merry Christmas, Tommy!"

"My name's Albert!" the young man shouted.

"Come here!" the German called. "We meet. We shake hands! You don't shoot – we don't shoot!"

Albert began to scramble over the top but Lieutenant Armstrong grabbed his belt and pulled him back. "It could be a trick."

"I never thought of that, sir."

"It's a risk you should not take."

"No, sir."

Then the German called. "It is Christmas! We shake hands!"

The young officer straightened his back. "I'll go and see what they want. If they shoot me then kill every German you can see. Cover me with your rifles."

"Yes, sir."

Lieutenant Clive Armstrong climbed into No Man's Land. A German searchlight flooded the frozen desert of mud and made the officer shield his eyes. He slowly unbuckled his pistol belt and let it fall to the ground. British troops in the trenches to his right and left raised their heads to watch.

One German stood up and walked out to meet him. When they reached one another they saluted. Then, as they shook hands, a cheer broke out from the British trenches and it was answered by a cheer from the enemy.

The Germans began singing 'Silent Night' while the two men in the middle seemed to be having a long and friendly conversation. When the carol was finished there was a silence in the night and a British soldier cried, "Can't you sing 'It's a Long Way to Tipperary'?"

"We will sing it for you, Tommy!" a German replied and the night was filled with the curious sound of German troops roaring out the British marching song. As the German singers struggled to sing 'God Save the King', Lieutenant Armstrong headed back to the British side and soldiers gathered round him. The officer was not much older than Private Albert Watson. His eyes were sparkling and his pale cheeks had pink spots in them. "I've spoken to their commander and agreed that we will have a truce for forty-eight hours."

The men cheered and Albert turned to Charlie Embleton. "That's good news, Charlie."

The older man shook his head. "Never seen anything like it in twenty years. It never happened in the Boer War. Anyone who tried it would have been shot."

"By the Boers?"

"Nah! By the British, you dummy. They can't have people going round making friends with the enemy."

"Why not?"

"Because, young feller, it would put us all out of a job," Charlie grinned. Then the grin faded. "Young Lieutenant Armstrong is taking a bit of a chance, talking to the enemy like that. They won't like it back at Headquarters."

"They're probably roasting a goose and stirring their Christmas puddings back at Headquarters. What do they care?" Albert asked.

"We'll see," Charlie shrugged. "We'll see."

As Christmas Eve slipped into Christmas morning the singing

began to fade. Charlie and Albert went to the rear trenches for some sleep and returned next morning. Albert looked cautiously over the top of the trench and saw a group of 20 Germans climb out with a football. They kicked it over the uneven ground and passed it to one another.

"I was a good footballer," Albert said.

"What? With legs like yours?" Charlie scoffed. "Never!"

"I was! Hey! I'll bet I could teach those Germans a trick or two."

"Go on then,"

"You what?"

Charlie climbed up to No Man's Land and called, "Albert Watson here's a star footballer. He says he could beat you with one foot tied behind his back!"

The Germans laughed and said, "We are the best football players in world."

Other sentries heard the cry and roared back, "Rubbish!" More British soldiers climbed up on to the crackling mud and someone said, "Eleven-a-side! Let's see how good you are!"

The Germans gathered into a group to choose their best 11 while the British troops did the same. Albert stood shyly in the group until Tom Taylor pointed to him. "Best right winger in the regiment." No one argued and Albert found himself stripping off his jacket and running on to the roughest football pitch the world had ever seen. A German officer had a whistle and acted as referee and timekeeper.

He blew and the match was under way.

For an hour there was no war. There was plenty of conflict though. Albert found that every time he ran forward with the ball he was kicked and tripped by a short, stocky German with a red face and thin, fair hair.

After one tackle Albert was sure his ankle was broken – only the heavy army boots saved him. The German booted the ball up the field where a tall officer glanced it with his head into the goal that was formed by rifles stuck in the hard earth.

The longer the game went on the slower the stocky German became. "Five minutes to go!" the referee cried.

The ball bounced and bobbled to Albert. He turned and saw his enemy charging towards him. The German's boots skidded over the earth in a slide that would break Albert's skinny legs. But he pushed the ball forward, jumped over the lunging German legs and raced towards the goal. The goalkeeper dived too soon, Albert waited and coolly slid the ball between the rifle-goalposts.

British soldiers cheered till their throats were raw and Albert had never felt so happy in his life. When the final whistle blew a few minutes later he was carried off the pitch on the shoulders of the happy British troops. The other players were shaking hands with their opponents.

Albert struggled to get his feet back on the ground then jogged back to the pitch. The stocky, red-faced German scowled at him. Suddenly he stuck out a fat arm. "Shake hand, Englishman. Good played."

"Good played, Fritz," Albert grinned.

The German allowed himself a small smile. It made him look much younger. Younger even than Albert. "Not Fritz. Hans. My name Hans."

"My name Albert. Good played Hans."

"Good played Albert."

They kept the handshake firm as they looked into one another's eyes for half a minute or more. "Good shoot," Hans said.

"Thanks," Albert replied and felt himself blushing.

Suddenly the German's eyes turned glassy and his face bleak. "Today shoot football. Tomorrow shoot guns."

Albert's head dropped. "Aye."

When he looked up Hans was marching back towards his trench. "Hans!" Albert cried.

The German stopped and turned.

"Good luck," Albert said. He recited the words from his memory as if they were some magic charm. "May God protect you and bring you home safe."

Hans gave a brief nod. "You too, Albert. You too."

World War I Christmas Truce

1. A Christmas truce, like the one in 1914, had been seen in many other wars. It was nothing new. But at first the British troops were suspicious about the appearance of Christmas trees. In many places their first reaction was to shoot them down. The Germans replaced them patiently and the British stopped firing.

2. There were several reports of football matches between the enemies. Some were organized and others were just friendly kick-abouts with 100 men joining in. Where the scores were recorded the most common result seems to have been Germany 3 Britain 2.

3. One British officer recognized a German soldier in No Man's Land during the truce. The German had been his barber in

F A C T F I L E

F A C T

F I L E

London before the war. He agreed to cut the English officer's hair and to shave some of the British soldiers. A German soldier who had performed in British theatres did a juggling act to entertain both sides.

4. In some trenches the enemy became almost too friendly. The German soldiers wanted to visit the British trenches. The captain in charge refused because he didn't want the Germans to see how weak his forces were because of illness and injuries. He allowed some of his men to meet the Germans half way and ordered the rest to march up and down the trenches to make it look as if they had a large number of defenders.

5. Some truces went on until New Year's Day but most ended after Boxing Day. In one part of the trenches the British politely told the Germans, "We will start shooting again at nine o'clock". The Germans called back, "Then we'll come over to your trenches – we'll be safer!" Many of the men found it hard to start fighting again. When their officers gave the order to shoot the soldiers replied, "We can't – they are good fellows and we can't". The officers replied, "If you don't start firing then we will – and it won't be at the Germans." The German troops had the same problem. For several days the British and Germans fired at one another without trying to hit. A soldier wrote, "We spent that day and the next wasting ammunition in trying to shoot the stars from the sky."

6. The commanders on both sides were furious when they heard about the Christmas truce. Talking in a friendly way to the enemy is a crime known as "fraternization". Normally a soldier guilty of fraternization would be punished. But at Christmas 1914 there were just too many men shaking hands with the enemy. If they punished them all then there would not be enough men left to fight! And orders from the governments insisted that the fight should go on. In time new men moved into the front-line trenches of both sides. These men had not taken part in the Christmas truce because they had been too far behind the front lines. The new men began the serious fighting and killing again.

7. As World War I grew more bitter, a Christmas truce like the one in 1914 was never seen again. The only time the firing stopped was to allow the enemy to send stretcher-bearers into No Man's Land to collect the dead and dying. There were plenty of both. Over eight million people died and 21 million were wounded. When the war ended on 11 November 1918, French Prime Minister Georges Clemenceau said to one of his generals, "We have won the war: now we have to win the peace, and it may be more difficult". He was right.

8. One German refused to step into No Man's Land and shake hands with the enemy during the Christmas 1914 truce. He said, "That sort of thing should not happen in war". He stayed in his dugout. As a result he never learned to make friends with the British and French enemies. This was a pity because the man's name was Corporal Adolf Hitler. Twenty years later he became leader of Germany and took them into a second, even more horrific, world war.

RESCUED

World War II was different. In a popular wartime film a vicar summed it up:

"This is not only a war of soldiers in uniforms. It is a war of the people – and it must be fought not only on the battlefields but in the cities and villages, in the factories and on the farms, in the homes and in the heart of every man, woman and child who loves freedom. Well, we have buried our dead but we shall not forget them. Instead they will inspire us with an unbreakable determination to free ourselves and those who come after us from the tyranny and terror that threaten to strike us down. This is a people's war. It is our war. We are the fighters."

The "fighters" included women like Michelle Alain. She lived in Belgium, which was occupied and ruled by German invaders. This is her story...

Date: September 1944
Place: Belgium
They called it the *Phantom Train* and I guess that we were the

102

ghosts. Fifteen hundred of us on the train, crammed into the airless trucks, 100 to each wagon. If we survived the journey to Germany then we'd be shot as soon as we arrived at the other end.

No one wept and no one complained. It was the risk we all knew we were taking when we joined the Resistance movement against the Germans.

"I don't mind dying," said the little man with wide blue eyes in an innocent face. "It's just a shame that we were so close to being rescued."

"A few hours," I nodded. "A day at the most. The Americans and British are almost here."

"They say they could hear their heavy guns," he said eagerly. "They can't be more than twenty miles away. Twenty miles. Maybe a few hours from safety. Such a shame."

"So you regret joining the Resistance?" I asked.

"No, no!" he said. "Better to be dead than ruled by Mister Hitler," he said cheerfully. "What do you say?"

"I agree. That's why I joined. Sometimes I felt like the cat who had nine lives. I have been so close to dying, so many times, that now I'm really going to die it seems unreal."

He chewed his lip and said, "I know we shouldn't talk about our work – I mean to say, I *could* be a German spy planted here to get your secrets from you. But you can talk to me about it if you wish."

"Thank you," I said. "And if you are a German spy then you can tell your masters that they will never win this war. They can kill our bodies but they'll never kill our spirit."

"Never," he agreed.

There was a stir in the truck and a whispered message ran around. "Someone has ripped the brakes out of the engine. We can't move!"

"Who would do such a dreadful thing?" a woman said, pretending to be shocked.

"It was the driver himself, they say!"

"A good man," someone said and everyone muttered in agreement. A delay like that only put off the hour of our death for a little while, but we welcomed it.

"I worked for Etienne in the Tegal network," I told my little friend. "I did a small job, crossing into France and taking false papers to British bomber pilots who'd crashed and wanted to escape. I did well and Etienne asked if I wanted to work for him."

"You said, 'Yes', of course?"

"I didn't even hesitate."

"Why?"

I sighed. "It sounds odd, but people do things for the strangest reasons. But my husband was all in favour of the Nazis ruling Belgium. He said they were 'efficient' and they would make us rich and happy, once the war was over. The trouble was I had learned to hate my husband! If *he* loved the Nazis then *I* would struggle against them."

"It must have been dangerous for you – working for the Resistance and living in the same house as a Nazi-lover?"

"No. At least I knew my enemy. Better than living in a house with someone pretending to love Belgium, but being a traitor to us! We have lost a few friends that way."

"True," the little man nodded.

"I became Etienne's secretary. At first I was typing messages, drawing sketch plans of German positions so we could photograph them and send the microfilm to Britain. Sketches like that helped to guide the British bombers by night and the American bombers by day."

The truck we were in shook suddenly. "They've attached a new locomotive," someone said. "Won't be long now." We all went silent and waited for the train to start moving. Nothing happened.

"I was always expecting to be caught," I told the man. "I remember cycling towards the office one day and seeing a black Citroën car parked in front of the block of flats next to us. The number on the car was 415-133."

"Gestapo, of course," the man said. "Gestapo always use 415 numbers."

"I couldn't turn round and cycle away. The officers had seen me. They would follow me. I had no choice. I had to go into the office. I got off the bike and hoped they didn't see how much it was shaking under my hands."

"They didn't?"

"They didn't. I ran up the stairs and told Etienne about the car. He said, 'The worst thing we can do is run away'. Someone in the office said we could leave one at a time. But that way we'd have been followed separately. We decided to give it half an hour to see what happened. After twenty minutes they drove off and we relaxed. I felt that one of my cat's lives had gone ... until I saw that the car had pulled on to a patch of waste ground and was sitting there. Watching. Maybe I wasn't a cat – maybe they were the cats and I was the mouse."

"You were suspected," the little man said. "You'd have to destroy all your papers."

"Easier said than done," I told him. "It was a clear blue day. Any smoke from burning papers would bring them running."

"Unless you could burn them very quickly," he said.

"We stuffed papers and photographs into the old cast-iron stove. Etienne made us empty our pockets. Then we put a match to the stove but we'd stuffed it too tight. The fire went out. We pulled half the charred paper out and tried again. The sky must have been black with the smoke. The next time I looked out of the window the Gestapo car had moved closer. They never left the car."

"Waiting for the knock on the door. That's the worst part," my friend said.

"No knock on the door," I said. "It was a ring on the bell! We froze! We were sure we would be shot down where we stood. Then the doorbell rang again, and Etienne told us, 'The Gestapo never ring twice. If you don't answer the first time they come in shooting.' I went over to the spy-hole in the door and squinted through it. I couldn't believe it! My husband was standing there!"

"He'd betrayed you to the Nazis?"

"No! He was just jealous because he thought I was spending too much time with my boss! Ha! It was the first time in five years that I was pleased to see him. I collected my handbag and went home with him like a good wife. The Gestapo watching must have known he was one of their supporters. They didn't try to stop us. I didn't know walking along a street could be so wonderful. Just being alive!"

My story was interrupted again by shouting from outside the truck. The message was passed along, "The replacement driver's had an accident now! Scalded himself with steam from a valve!"

"Another accident?" someone asked.

"I doubt it," came the reply. "Doesn't look like they'll ever get us to the death camp."

"Then they'll simply shoot us here," I said.

"They can't," a young woman near me said. "There are Red Cross observers at the station. Any German who takes a shot at us will become a war criminal when the war is over. They'll be executed themselves. And the Germans know the end can't be far away."

We settled down again to wait. A few more hours' delay was all we needed, just a few more hours. It was more than we could hope for.

"Did you help many pilots to escape?" the little man asked me.

"About twenty. But we had some close shaves. Once we saw a British plane come down near a farm and we raced there on our bicycles. We helped the pilot into a barn but the Germans arrived in a truck just a minute later. We didn't have time to hide him. '*Englander! Englander!*' they were shouting. I acted stupid and pointed across the field. There was a pile of white fertilizer powder two fields away. From the barn it was just a white shape. 'Parachute!' I said and I pointed to the white shape. They all rushed off to the fertilizer and by the time they came back the pilot was safely hidden away."

"The Germans must have been furious," the man chuckled.

"They came storming back to the farmhouse," I told him. "Then they saw a shape hidden by a white cloth. They didn't risk pulling the cloth off – it could have been an airman with a pistol. So they fired a clip of machine-gun bullets into it."

"They killed him?"

"No! It wasn't the airman. It was the carcass of a pig that was salted for the winter. The white cloth was just to keep the flies off," I laughed.

It was the last time I laughed for a while. The message was passed back that a third engine driver had been brought to the train with three armed guards ready to shoot him if he failed to move the train. As the locomotive jumped into life it sent a thump through the coupling that seemed to go straight to my stomach.

"We're going backwards," someone said.

"The driver has to. We're facing the wrong way. When we reach the points he'll go off on the branch line to Germany."

We listened to the steady clank of the train over the rails, then the loud clatter as we crossed the points. The train didn't stop. In fact it seemed to be picking up speed. "If we keep going like this we'll be in France in half an hour!"

"We're going the wrong way!" everyone agreed.

The train finally slowed and coasted into a station. "Malines," a man said looking through a crack in the door. "The Germans are trying to fill the engine with water. They're determined to get us back to Germany."

I squeezed against the door and looked through the gap between the sliding door and the side of the truck. A tubby man in a uniform was talking to an angry German officer. "Sabotage!" he was saying. "The water tanks have been emptied!"

The German officer pushed him out of the way and started snapping orders at his men. In half an hour they were filling buckets of water from a tap and passing them in a chain to the engine. We were already 12 hours late. If only we could have had another 12 hours the Allies could reach us and save us. The train staff were doing their best. But the Germans were stubborn – they were going to get us to Germany or bust.

It was dark by the time we pulled back into Brussels station.

The train was pulled into a siding. Someone came round with a bucket of water but no food. At least the open door let in a little fresh, cooler air. "We'll be in Germany by morning," the little man sighed. "It was a great adventure while it lasted."

"We still aren't moving," I told him. And it seemed there were so many trains passing through the station on the way to Germany there was no room for us.

"It's the German troops on the run. They're getting their wounded back to Germany before they deal with us."

"There's still hope for us, then?" I asked. Hope is the cruellest thing. I could have coped with the idea of dying if it was all over quickly. Suddenly I found I couldn't bear the thought of surviving and dying later. I cried silently in the darkness and some time during the night I fell asleep.

I awoke when the little man shook me. He'd taken his coat off and thrown it over me, though he must have been cold himself. "What is it?" I asked. Weak daylight was creeping through the cracks in the wagon panels.

"They are opening the wagons," he said.

"Are we in Germany, then?"

"No," he said. "The train hasn't moved from Brussels."

"So they'll shoot us here, then."

He took my hand and squeezed it. "Maybe not."

The heavy footsteps reached the door of our wagon and stopped. There was a clatter of bolts being slid back and the soft grey daylight made us blink. A German officer with a stone-pale face glared into the truck. "Get out!" he ordered.

We climbed out slowly and stiffly, the strong helping the weak. We joined the others from the *Phantom Train* in a goods yard. The officer got his men to herd us into a square. We heard the clicking of the safety catches coming off the rifles and machine-guns. A man in a soft brown hat and navy coat walked quietly behind the German officer. He had an armband with a red cross on it. He said nothing.

The officer spoke to us in bad French. It wasn't helped by the fact that he was spluttering with anger. "You are murderers and traitors. You have fought against the German Reich but you have done it as cowards. You have not fought in uniforms. You have fought as spies in plain clothes. The penalty for this is death. You all know this."

A thousand pairs of eyes stared back at him silently. Suddenly the booming sound of heavy guns disturbed the peace of the morning. They were much closer than they had been the night before. The German officer and his men looked around nervously and began to back away towards a train that was building up steam on the line next to ours. It looked as if the plan was to climb on to the train and shoot us as they pulled away. People huddled closer – it would only make us an easier target, of course, but there was a great comfort in having someone friendly near when you are going to die.

The sky over Brussels was glowing red as the Hall of Justice began to burn. "Cowards and traitors!" the Gestapo officer screamed as he climbed on to an open truck as his train began to pull away.

His men lowered their weapons and settled into the jolting train to make themselves comfortable for the journey back to Germany. A journey that we should have made 24 hours before.

We could see his face filled with hatred and rage till it disappeared in the distance. We were still too stunned to move. Sometimes it is harder to believe good luck than to believe bad.

The streets of Brussels were full of dazed Belgians unable to take in what was happening.

At four o'clock that afternoon the Allied tanks rolled into the town and we knew we were truly free. But for the 1,500 people on that train the miracle wasn't the freedom – it was the fact that we were alive at all.

They called us heroes and heroines of the Resistance. But the truth is the heroes were the unknown men of the Belgian railways who'd done everything they could to make sure that train never left. The train that went nowhere. The train that became known as the *Phantom Train*.

Resistance

Michelle Alain was one of the lucky ones to escape. Many others were just as brave but died resisting German rule in their homelands...

1. Violette Szabo lost her husband when he was killed fighting for Britain against the Germans. She volunteered to join the French Resistance movement to get her revenge. She was eventually captured after a shoot-out with German soldiers; she held back several German troops with her machine-gun while another Frenchman with her escaped. She refused to betray the names of her friends in the Resistance even though she was tortured. Eventually Violette was sent to Ravensbruck concentration camp where she was shot.

2. Odette Samson was parachuted into enemy France to work with the Resistance. The Germans managed to put a spy into her group and she was betrayed and captured. She survived torture and being locked away for days in a darkened room to terrify her. She explained later that she'd been blind for over three years when she was a child, so she wasn't afraid of the dark! She survived Ravensbruck camp and was released by the American Army in 1945.

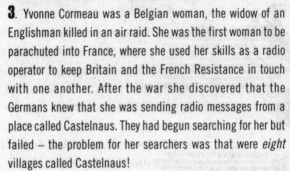

3. Yvonne Cormeau was a Belgian woman, the widow of an Englishman killed in an air raid. She was the first woman to be parachuted into France, where she used her skills as a radio operator to keep Britain and the French Resistance in touch with one another. After the war she discovered that the Germans knew that she was sending radio messages from a place called Castelnaus. They had begun searching for her but failed – the problem for her searchers was that were *eight* villages called Castelnaus!

4. Yvette Tranberg helped run an escape route in France. Money for the scheme came from a man who sold nuts and bolts to the German army – but the nuts and bolts didn't fit each other; the Germans were paying for the escape route and getting nothing in return! Messages were passed in newspapers – a pinprick was put under certain letters to spell out the words. When the war was coming to an end Yvette watched German torturers being rounded up and machine-

F A C T   F I L E

gunned; at the time she watched quite happily. Later she was horrified to realize how cruel the war had made her.

5. Andrée de Jongh helped her husband in the French Resistance but they were betrayed by a Belgian and arrested. On her way to a concentration camp with 40 other women she was warned not to sit on the floor of the railway wagon. It was dusted with chalk and the chalk gave off a poisonous gas that caused its victims to suffocate. She survived the concentration camp – the cold and the lack of food – but had to walk for two weeks to get to safety when the war ended. At last she reached Paris where she hoped to be reunited with her husband after a year. Instead she discovered that he'd died on the first day after their capture.

6. Joke Fulmer helped the Dutch Resistance by delivering their secret newspaper. She was betrayed by a boy in the Dutch Gestapo and imprisoned. She said that a paper clip kept her going through six weeks of being locked up alone. She used it to scratch a calendar on the wall, make figures from the wire and write poems. "With a paper clip everything is all right," she said. When the Russians freed her she weighed just five-and-a-half stone (35kg).

Women had led quiet and unexciting lives before the war. Despite all the dangers and hardships they missed the excitement when the war ended. You might have expected them to say it was the worst time of their lives. Many did say that, but a surprising number agreed with the Women's Air Force member who said, "It took years to settle down to life after the war. I had changed and no longer spoke the same language as my family. Life after the war seemed slow, dull and pointless. We had seen dreadful sights and lost many friends. Our responsibilities had been great but it had been exciting and we had worked as a team. I wouldn't have missed it for anything."

She was not alone…

EPILOGUE

Date: July 1996
Place: Newcastle upon Tyne

World War I, from 1914 to 1918, killed millions of people. Its brutality shocked the world. Politicians swore that it would never happen again.

Eighty years after the bloodiest battle, the Battle of the Somme in 1916, most of the fighters were dead. The ones who survived the war – and survived the war that followed – had died of old age. But the very few who lived on were aged around 100.

A young reporter was sent to interview George Sewell and was surprised to find a friendly, rosy-cheeked man with bright eyes and a cheerful smile.

"I'm Anna," she said. "I wanted to talk to you about World War I."

"Sit down, lass," the old man said, and waved at a chair with his walking stick.

"I thought I'd do an article about the trenches, the gas attacks, the mud and the disease," she said.

"Why?" the man asked.

"To show the horrors of war. To let people see how evil war is."

"Why?"

"So they'll never do it again!" she laughed. "You've seen it

118

close up. You know how terrible it was. I was hoping you could tell the readers."

The old soldier frowned. "I'm a hundred years old. The war was eighty years ago. But if you asked me what was the strongest memory of my whole life, then I'd have to say it was the Great War."

The young woman nodded eagerly. "Because it was so horrific."

He looked at her from under his thick, grey eyebrows. "Do you want to put words into my mouth, young lady?"

"Of course not!" she smiled. "But I've read about the trenches. It was dreadful."

"It was," the old soldier nodded. "But you should write a bit about the good side."

Her mouth fell open a little. "But there wasn't a good side," she said.

"How do you know?" he asked.

"There can't have been," she argued.

"But you forget that people are strange creatures. The harder their lives, then the more they pull together. Imagine a bunch of lads like me joining up in 1914. We worked in shops and pits and offices and building sites. Going off to fight together was a great adventure," the old man remembered.

"But when you set out you didn't know how bad it would be," the reporter said.

"That's what I'm trying to explain. The worse it got the closer we got to our mates. A friendship made in war is the strongest friendship I've ever known. There's a lot to be said for that. And the more we suffered the more we appreciated the simple things like a good meal or a hot cup of tea. Are you going to tell your readers that?" he asked.

"It's an interesting thought," the young woman sniffed. It wasn't the interview she'd come to get. Her editor wouldn't be pleased.

"You want me to say war is a terrible thing? Right! I'll say it! War is a terrible thing. But it teaches you a lot about life, and you learn a lot about people. You also find out a lot about *yourself*. You grow up quick in a war. You find out what you're made of."

"If you survive," the reporter said.

"If you survive," the old man nodded. "I made a lot of friends in the trenches. I lost a lot more. They thought they were risking their lives to make a better world. Maybe they were foolish to think that. Maybe you think they failed. But I don't think you should go *writing* that they were foolish and failed, do you?"

The young woman folded her notebook. "It's been good to talk to you, Mr Sewell," she said with a tight smile.

"When you get to my age it's good to talk to anyone," he replied.

She rose and walked out of the old people's home, across the road and past the soot-stained war memorial. George watched her stop and read the inscription and the hundred names of the men from the village who'd died in the two wars. He hoped she'd understand the inscription. He couldn't see it so well now but he knew it by heart:

They shall not grow old, as we that are left grow old.
Age shall not weary them, nor the years condemn.

At the going down of the sun and in the morning
We will remember them.[1]

There were more recent names carved into the dull stone. Soldiers who'd died in the Falklands War and in Northern Ireland.

Underneath there was a space. It was almost as if it was set aside for new names in the future.

1. From the poem "For the Fallen" by Laurence Binyon

DON'T MISS THESE GRIPPING CRIME STORIES

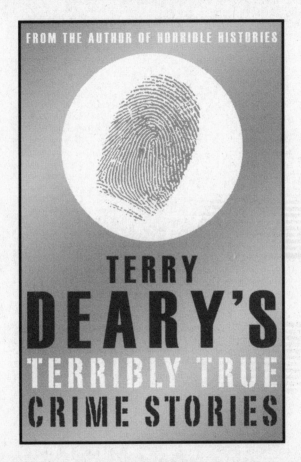

FROM THE AUTHOR OF HORRIBLE HISTORIES

TERRY
DEARY'S
TERRIBLY TRUE
CRIME STORIES

They're guaranteed to bring out
the super sleuth in you!

DON'T MISS THESE GRIPPING SPY STORIES

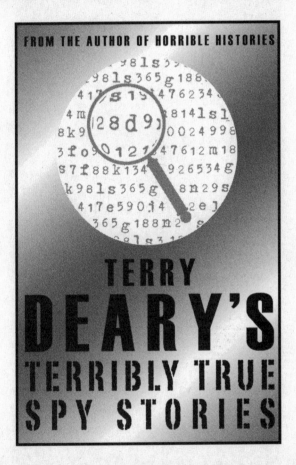

FROM THE AUTHOR OF HORRIBLE HISTORIES

TERRY
DEARY'S
TERRIBLY TRUE
SPY STORIES

They're guaranteed to bring out
the armchair agent in you!

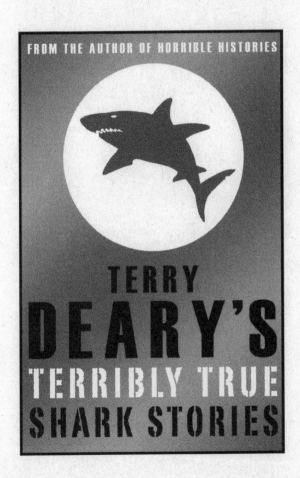